STO

ACPL ITEM
DISCARDED

ANNEX

ANNEX

Y0-BWS-130

3-21-62

KNOW YOUR ENEMY

KNOW Your Enemy

by

DELIA MARES

illustrated by

V. Hollan

Second Edition

GULF PUBLISHING COMPANY
HOUSTON, TEXAS

KNOW YOUR ENEMY

Copyright© 1961 by Gulf Publishing Company, Houston, Texas. All rights reserved. Printed in the United States of America. This book, or portions thereof, may not be reproduced in any form without permission of the publishers.

Library of Congress Catalog Card No. 61-14522.

Acknowledgments

Since the first edition of *Know Your Enemy* was published in 1952 the threat of Communist power to societies which respect individual worth and freedom has increased enormously. So has the task of preparing a short, factual and comprehensive account of the growing danger to the Free World.

The Communist area of operations has expanded to cover the entire world and beyond; the Communist military arsenal has been vastly enlarged; Communist propaganda techniques and activities add ever new dimensions to the challenge. This book was written especially for that generation in the Free World—the generation of my sons—which will bear the brunt of this challenge.

1181934

Among the dozens of people who have assisted me by criticisms and suggestions I am particularly indebted to several experts who read the manuscript in various stages and discussed it with me. These included: Dr. Carl Friedrich, Professor of Government at Harvard University; Joseph Harrison, Overseas News Editor of the *Christian Science Monitor;* Charles Vetter Jr., Training Director of the United States Information Agency; Tadeusz A. Pawlowicz, formerly of the Polish Foreign Service and now on the staff of Radio Free Europe; Dr. Joseph Nogee, Associate Professor of Political Science at the University of Houston.

For the final organization and emphasis, however, the responsibility is entirely mine.

Delia Mares

Foreword

by

DR. JAMES R. KILLIAN, JR.

Chairman of President Kennedy's
Foreign Intelligence Advisory Board

Chairman of the Corporation,
Massachusetts Institute of Technology

Former Special Assistant to President
Eisenhower for Science and Technology

Today when the United States is carrying the awesome responsibility for the leadership and defense of the Free World, it is of urgent importance that Americans understand both the threat we face and the requirements this responsibility imposes on us.

We and our institutions face increasingly severe tests and mortal danger, threatened as we are by dictators who rule one third of the world and are determined to rule still more of mankind. "These rulers," as the President's Commission on National Goals emphasized, "seek the 'peace' of a Communist-oriented world, in which freedom is suppressed and the individual permanently subordinated. Supporting their aim are the Soviet Union's great and swiftly growing strength, the industrial and military progress and potential of Red China, a great capacity for political organization and propaganda, and the specious appeal of Communist doctrine to peoples eager for rapid escape from poverty."

This Communist threat together with the unrest and turbulence troubling the world today require of us Americans a steady striving to achieve higher performance in all aspects of our national life; every part of our society must seek to be vigorous, adaptable, forward-thrusting, and of the highest quality. Only by possessing this measure of quality, strength, and elan, and having other peoples know we possess them, can we be sure of maintaining our leadership in the world arena. By our own example of the strength and effectiveness of a free people's government, we must make clear that a free society is a great and good society always growing better and thus one worthy of leadership. Along with this determination to maintain and advance a great society, must go the willingness, the skill, and the toughness to maintain great military strength and a sound rate of economic growth.

These responsibilities and requirements cannot be met by a citizenry of limited awareness and inadequately mobilized and trained intelligence. They *can* be met by citizens who govern their affairs by the understanding that the "power of nations rests upon the power of intelligence" and public understanding.

At times I become discouraged by the widespread indifference to these requirements of the cold war, of survival, and world leadership. Among other things I become troubled by the lack of a clear, penetrating understanding of the threat America faces. America, of course, rejects and detests Communism, but it does not always understand the wellsprings of Communist power, policy, and maneuver, and thus our rejection and resistance are not as skillfully effective as they might be. Sometimes our lack of understanding of the intrinsic nature of what we scorn and reject permits us, in the words of Clinton Rossiter, to be "tempted or bullied by the fierce pressure of events into aping the habits of thought we scorn." In fighting Communism we run the hazard of using methods dangerous to the liberties of free men. While avoiding this temptation, we need at the same time to make sure that we as a people have the insight and understanding to fight Communism effectively in the realm of ideas. We must have the intellectual, ideological sureness to prevent the Communist from getting away with specious ideas and propaganda. Communism is one of the most impressive of all examples of the power of ideas, and we must be sure that we mobilize to oppose it with ideas—and a faith—still more compelling.

These random observations are prompted by reading Mrs. Mares' vade mecum on Communism. I am glad that she has brought her book up to date for it is an admirably terse and lucid description of the true nature of our enemy, the good along with the wicked. It can contribute importantly in fulfilling the public's need to know and to understand the threat with which we must deal. By understanding this threat, we have a better chance of protecting ourselves successfully—and a better chance to do this by peaceful means. Mrs. Mares has performed a public service by making available this new edition which many readers can use rewardingly as they face the problems of a divided world.

Dr. James R. Killian, Jr.

Cambridge, Mass.
July, 1961

Contents

Maps and Illustrations

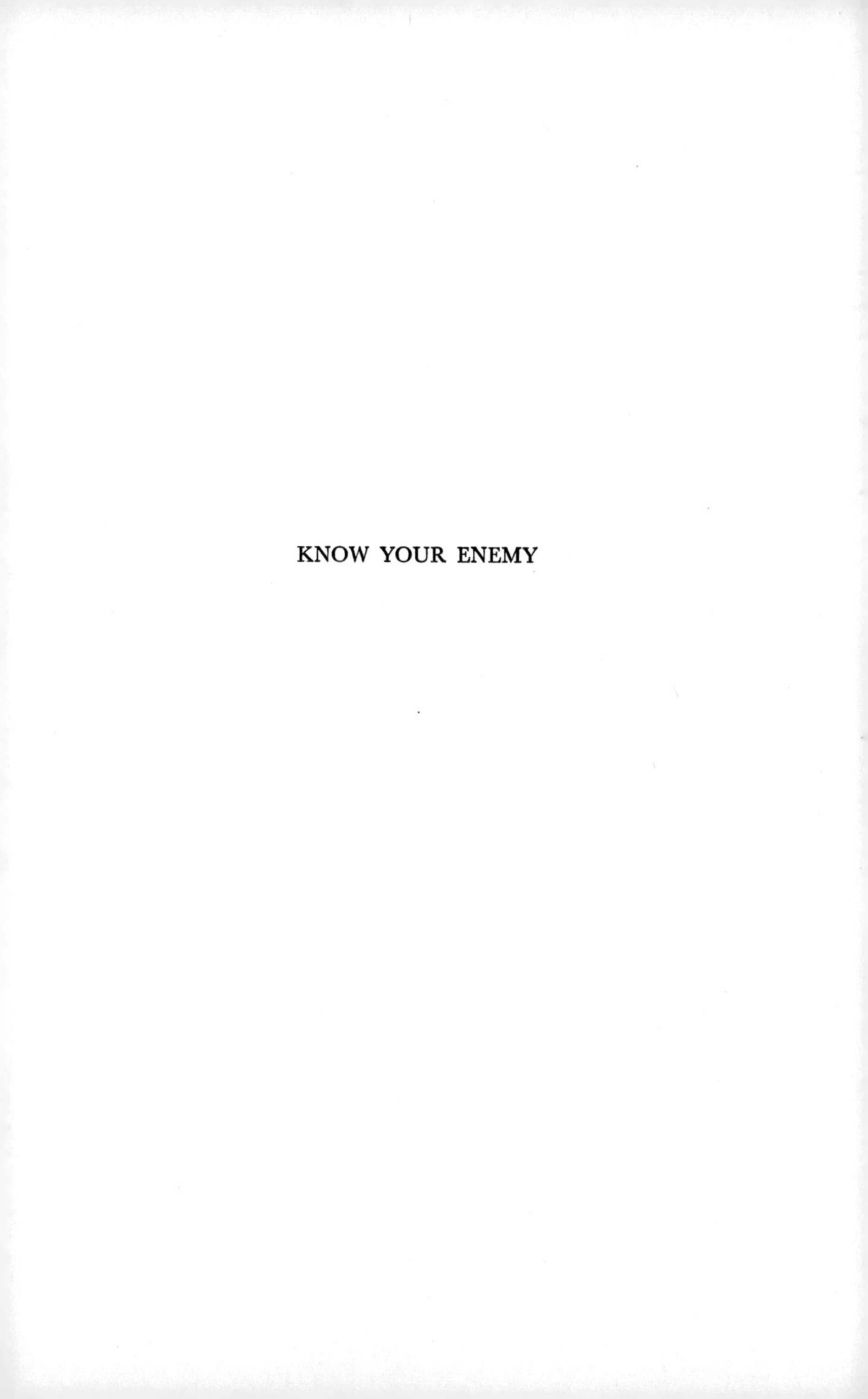

KNOW YOUR ENEMY

Introduction

by

WILLIAM J. DONOVAN

In writing *Know Your Enemy* Mrs. Mares has done a great service to the American people. Her book provides a concise exposition of the development of the Communist Party and its tactics of subversion.

Pointing out that the teachings of Marx as refined and explained by Lenin and Stalin constitute the "bible" of all Communist thinking and action today, Mrs. Mares devotes the major part of her book to an analysis and description of the life and teachings of these three "architects" of revolutionary Communism, and the role which they played in the development of the Communist state in Russia since the turn of the century. Her detailed analysis of the means employed by Stalin to perfect his absolute control over the lives of the Russian people and her lucid description of Soviet foreign policy furnish us with a valuable insight into the Soviet techniques of subversion employed so successfully on a global basis since World War II.

The author shows us that the discipline of the Communist Party is more like that of an army than that of any other political party. We should not underestimate its organization, its temper and its vigor. We face a ruthless and tenacious foe whose tactics may change even to temporary retreat but whose objective remains the same—a world empire.

The author helps us to comprehend the character of this war of maneuver which the Kremlin wages against us in every target country using the 5th column and the Communist Party as Stalin's Army of Occupation.

This book should be read by every citizen. All high school students especially should read it in order to prepare themselves to meet a danger which will challenge their future. Against such a foe we must exercise sustained effort perhaps for many years.

An imaginative and affirmative American foreign policy can be reached only by a realistic appraisal of the aims and objectives of the Soviet Union. The author gives us this appraisal.

—William J. Donovan

September 25, 1952

1

Who Is The Enemy?

Ask any American "What is the greatest threat to your country and you?" and he will answer "Communism." Ask what it is and how we should combat it and each will give you a different answer. Meanwhile, the Communists of the world are centrally controlled, able to direct their power and propaganda at one place today, at another tomorrow, wherever the United States and the Free World seem weakest.

What can an American do?

First of all, he must know his enemy.

But this is not easy. The faces of Communism are many. Marx and his friend Engels, Lenin, Stalin, Malenkov and Khrushchev, Mao Tse Tung, the men behind Castro, and who knows how many others? Since the *Communist Manifesto* of 1848 Communism has had over a century to grow and change. It is a dictatorship and a tyranny. Dictatorships have come and gone, maintained by physical power and by centralized control. Today's Communism commands the physical power of nuclear weapons and the centralized control of the Communist Party over every aspect of life. But in addition it has another kind of power which past tyrannies never imagined, for modern methods of communication have given Communists the power to influence men's minds.

Americans must understand how Communists use this power over their own subjects and toward those they hope to win—and against those like ourselves whom they wish to destroy. The first step in knowing our enemy is to understand the Communists' use, misuse and abuse of words.

By using such invented terms as "revisionism," the ruling group of Communists can condemn any Communists who do not agree with them. Russia has accused Yougoslavia of "revisionism."

By the distorted use of familiar words such as "peace," "democracy," and "morality," they create a fog of confusion to hide their purposes. For the Communists, "peace" is the condition where Communism has triumphed; "democracy" is rule by the Communist Party; "morality" is whatever promotes the goals of Communism.

By misuse of the words "capitalism," "colonialism," and "imperialism" they attack us. To these and many other words Communists give their own set of meanings by which they justify to themselves and (they hope) to others whatever the Communist rulers choose to do.

Communist use of the words "communism" and "socialism" is also part of their plan of confusion. Let us begin by understanding the different meanings of these words so that we will not fall into this Communist trap.

How Communism Got Its Name

Men have always been troubled by extremes of rich and poor and have tried many times to make everyone equal by setting up communities where property was owned in common. Various groups of people in Europe and America tried this during the nineteenth century. These groups were called "communes" and the common ownership of property was called "communism." They existed as independent idealistic units as long as they had able leadership, but when their leaders died or were followed by less able men, the groups faded out, one by one. They left behind them just one thing, the word "communism" to suggest the vague idea that, if all property could be owned in common, everyone would be equal. The word and the idea were familiar to German thinkers in the middle of the nineteenth century—among them, Karl Marx. He proposed a totally different form of communism which he claimed was based on "scientific" principles.

What interested Marx, however, was not so much how "communism" was to be worked out in practical life, as how it was to replace capitalism. His emphasis was on revolution. This is what attracted Lenin to Marx's ideas. As we shall see, the Communism of Lenin, Stalin, Khrushchev and Mao Tse Tung bears no resemblance whatever to the idealistic communes of the European and American experiments.

What is Socialism?

In December 1960 the Communist parties of the world issued a 20,000 word document attacking the United States and its allies as "imperialists" and referring to themselves as the "socialist camp." In the same year Willy Brandt, the anti-Communist mayor of West Berlin, announced that he would be the Socialist candidate for President of West Germany. Americans cannot be blamed for confusion over the meaning of the word "socialism."

Marx, who made the word popular, meant by "socialism," government ownership and control of such essential parts of the economy as factories, railroads and banks. His writings convinced many people that such government ownership and control would bring about more justice and less poverty among men. About the year 1900, these people split into two groups. One group was the Socialists and Social Democrats of western Europe who wanted to bring about government ownership by the free choice of all the people. The others were the Bolsheviks of Russia led by Lenin who wanted to bring it about by revolution and the dictatorship of a small group.

The Socialists have always respected and supported the safeguards of political freedom—free elections, representative governments and freedom of speech. The Bolsheviks (later called the Communists) have always ruled by the dictatorship of the Party, with no free elections, no representative government and no freedom of speech.

Today's Communist leaders call their system "socialism," knowing well that to the many countries with only limited resources, "socialism" seems a way to achieve more justice and less poverty for all. In the Communist Party newspaper *Pravda* for November 26, 1955 there appeared the following quotation of a remark made by the Russian leader Khrushchev when he was visiting India.

"The Prime Minister of India, Mr. Nehru, declared that India would also take the socialist road. . . . Of course, we have a different conception of socialism."

What Nehru meant by "socialism" was what the Social Democrats of West Germany, the British Labor Party and most of our allies mean by "socialism"—a large measure of government ownership and control of the economy carried out by political parties chosen in free elections. In many free countries the Socialist parties have been voted into office and later voted out again.

What Khrushchev and the Communists mean by "socialism," however, is dictatorship by a self-chosen and permanent group of rulers, the Communist Party, over every aspect of people's lives.

The Faces of Communism

Of the many faces of Communism, a few are known everywhere. Karl Marx, 1818-1883, was a German scholar, writer and philosopher who worked out the ideas on which present-day Communism is based. Communists have placed Marx's *Das Kapital* and his other writings in the same position in which Christians have placed the Bible and Moslems the Koran, as the essential truth about the world which may be interpreted but never seriously criticized or questioned.

Lenin, 1870-1924, was the Russian who organized and trained the Communist Party as a small, disciplined, ruthless group determined to bring about a Marxist revolution in Russia by any and all means. After years of exile abroad, Lenin returned to Russia in 1917 to lead the Bolshevik Party in setting up the Soviet state, the Union of Soviet Socialist Republics—usually referred to as the U.S.S.R. Lenin's writings have been as important as those of Marx in providing the bases of Communist theory and practice. Everything Communist leaders do, they try to justify as "Marxism-Leninism."

Stalin, 1879-1953, fastened the control of the Communist Party upon every aspect of life in Russia. He developed Russian industry to the point of making atomic and hydrogen weapons. He promoted and directed Communist Parties all over the world in creating unrest and in spying for the U.S.S.R. During his rule Communist leaders worked out a technique for taking over countries from within which brought all of Eastern Europe under Soviet control. He ruled his own country by force and terror, keeping an Iron Curtain between his subjects and the outside world.

Khrushchev, who became the most powerful leader of the Soviet Union after Stalin's death, enlarged Communist strategy and goals. By offers of trade and aid to new countries, by personal meetings with the world's leaders, by various kinds of exchanges, he hopes to persuade others to become Communists. He has skillfully combined threats of nuclear warfare with offers of "peaceful co-existence,"—on his own terms.

Mao Tse Tung, Communist ruler of China, added 650 million Chinese to the strength of Communism.

Who are these men, and what is their danger to us?

KARL MARX 1818--1883

2

Karl Marx

Karl Marx is the principal philosopher of Communism. He was born in the German Rhineland of a well-educated Jewish family which had become Christian. Marx's father was considered the leading lawyer of the city of Trier, and Marx's wife came from a well-to-do family in the same city. From his teens Marx was determined to give his life to helping his fellowmen and to lessening the injustices and miseries he saw around him. His newspaper articles and pamphlets were suppressed by the government of Prussia and in 1849 he was expelled from Prussian territory.

After a short stay in France he took refuge in England where he lived and wrote freely for the rest of his life. He made very little money from his writing but depended on others for help, first on his wife's family, then on his friend and coworker, Friedrich Engels. The latter was the son of a wealthy manufacturer who owned factories in Germany and in Manchester, England. The English factory was managed by Engels and its profits supported him and the Marx family for many years.

Trouble stalked the Marx family. Several children died and Marx himself suffered frequent painful illnesses. Both his personal misfortunes and his idealistic nature made him deeply sympathetic with the factory workers, many of whom at that time were little better off than slaves. Child labor, crowded slums, inhumanly long hours wrecked hundreds of lives. These evils distressed other people besides Marx, and through trade unions and protective legislation conditions were beginning to be improved. Marx worked for some of these reforms, but he was primarily a student, intent on finding the causes of these evils so that they might be completely wiped out. From his researches in history he developed a theory about why these injustices existed, then a revolutionary program for changing them. Both his theory of history and his call to revolution are accepted without question by every Communist.

Karl Marx

Every writer reflects the society in which he lives. Writers like Marx, who try to interpret their society and predict its future, are more influenced by their surroundings than they themselves realize. Americans who would understand Marx and, through him, the thinking of present-day Communists, must understand something of the nineteenth-century European world in which Marx lived. That world differed in two outstanding respects from the world of modern Americans.

In the first place it was a world which was divided by sharp class lines. The sons of working people could not expect to be anything but working men, whereas the sons of rich or noble families would automatically inherit their wealth and position. Resentment against this system brought thousands of Europeans to America, to help build a society where their children could advance according to their ability and effort, rather than be bound for life in the class to which their parents belonged. Marx never came to America and never knew a society like ours, where there is always room at the top for hard work and brains. As a matter of fact, the class system in which Marx grew up has been the rule throughout history—even to the present day. It is the United States and the English-speaking dominions like Canada which are the exceptions. The Marxist-trained Communist today can find millions of people all over the world who feel as imprisoned in their class as did the Europeans in Marx's nineteenth century.

The second outstanding difference between Marx's world and ours has to do with the influence of certain thinkers. Marx was really a professor without a job or a classroom who tried to explain the views of those he thought had the truest interpretation of history. Marx's chief guide was the German philosopher Hegel, who had worked out a pattern for human development which Marx found entirely convincing. According to Hegel, human development always takes place according to the following pattern:

1. Thesis. Every movement in history proceeds uninterruptedly along its course until it is challenged by

2. Antithesis, an opposite movement which has been developing within or besides the first movement. These two clash and after a period of struggle emerges

3. Synthesis, which is neither the first nor the second but a combination of the best features of both.

Both Hegel and later Marx believed that the whole of history could be explained in terms of the (1) thesis, (2) the antithesis, (3) the synthesis; and they called this process the dialectic. To this day every Communist shares this rigid view of history and the propagandists for Soviet Russia refer to it frequently. It is scarcely necessary to say that historians and philosophers of the Free World do not believe that any such fixed pattern explains the complex and ever-changing actions of individual human beings. However, the idea of such a fixed pattern does appeal to people who want a mathematical explanation of non-mathematical problems. It appealed to Marx who was a serious student of mathematics, and Marx applied it to human situations to try to explain the reasons for poverty and injustice.

The "Class Struggle"

Marx's view of history, therefore, grew out of Europe's class society and Hegel's explanation of history. Americans should understand it because the Communists' whole program of world revolution is built on Marx's teachings about the past, present, and future. Marx explains the past as formed by the efforts of various classes to get economic power and to keep it for themselves. There is a distinct pattern of how this process operates, which has repeated itself again and again in history. First a small group in the community obtains control of the ways other people earn their living; then a group immediately below the first group becomes strong enough to demand admission to the ruling group or to overthrow it in a violent struggle (class-war). Having gained power, this group in turn becomes oppressors and, in turn, must be overthrown.

Marx used the example of the French Revolution of 1789-1793 to illustrate this process. The feudal nobility and the monarchy were ruling France in 1789 (Thesis). Their power and privileges were challenged by the rising merchants and business men of the towns, called by Marx and other historians the bourgeoisie (from the French, bourgeois, or townsman). (Antithesis). Finding themselves unable to obtain all the rights and privileges they desired by using peaceful means alone, the bourgeoisie joined with the peasants to overthrow the nobility and execute the king, taking the ruling power for themselves (Synthesis). Thus, they became a new ruling class, whom Marx regarded as oppressors of the next class below them, the industrial working class, or proletariat. According to Marx, only an uprising of the working class would force the bourgeoisie to give up the power they had taken from the nobility.

Capitalism as Seen by Marx

When Marx turned from his examination of the past to the world around him, he saw in England and other European countries the early stages of a capitalist society. In Marx's terms, the bourgeoisie, having seized power from the nobility, were now owing and operating the factories and other business enterprises in which the miserable workers were slaving for their oppressors. As any American who is familiar with the novels of Charles Dickens knows, dreadful conditions prevailed in those early factory towns and workshops. Some of these evils were no doubt caused by the selfishness of the factory owners and managers; on the other hand, part of the trouble was certainly due to the crowds of country people who poured into the cities seeking work, where as yet there were no houses or public institutions to care for such numbers.

At that time the great humanitarian movements had not yet taken shape, for society as a whole did not yet accept responsibility for the unfortunate. There was little organized charity or public welfare. But even in Marx's day trade unions had begun to form through which the workers could demand decent wages and working conditions. Enlightened factory owners were themselves helping improve conditions. Laws restricting working hours were passed during Marx's life-time. While Marx did try, toward the end of his life, to encourage some of these efforts at reform, he still believed that improvement could be brought about most effectively only through a revolution in which the industrial workers, or proletariat, took over power from their oppressors, the capitalists or bourgeoisie.

What Marx Thought About Human Behavior

Before examining further Marx's prophecy of future revolution, which is the heart and soul of modern Communist doctrine, it is important to understand what Marx thought about human motives—the reasons why men act as they do. Perhaps because of his own unhappy life, Marx's view of human beings was pessimistic and bitter. He held that everything men do or think is determined by what class they belong to and by the interests of that class. Not just the manner in which they earn their living, but what political party they support, how they educate their children, what religion they believe in, all these are determined by the position of their particular class in society. Government itself, he thought is simply the tool of the ruling class, which uses government to maintain and increase its power over the other classes in the country.

Marx's view of human nature is contrary to the teachings of all great religions that man can learn to care for his fellow men regardless of their position in society. It is also contrary to the findings of modern psychology that men have many different reasons for their actions—some selfish, some unselfish, some conscious, some unconscious. This view led Marx to regard all capitalists as selfish, grasping individuals who would wring every penny of work from their wretched workers, while—he thought—the working class, not having the temptations of property, would be entirely virtuous. Private property was the root of all human evil. To Americans who do not think in class terms and who realize that all men have both good and bad within them, this Marxist—and Communist—view will seem ridiculous. However, it does appeal to many hungry and hopeless people in other parts of the world and to some who are looking for rapid change.

The name given Marx's interpretation of man is "materialism," because he claimed that men acted chiefly according to their material interests.

He combined "materialism" with Hegel's "dialectical" interpretation of history to form the framework of Communism—"dialectical materialism." To a Communist, dialectical materialism is as much a religious faith as is Christianity to a Christian, Judaism to a Jew or Islam to a Moslem. In the educational systems of Russia and Eastern Europe, dialectical materialism as interpreted by Marx and Lenin has taken the place of religion. In China, dialectical materialism as interpreted by Marx, Lenin and Mao Tse Tung has replaced Confucianism and Buddhism.

The Future According to Marx

Marx believed that dialectical materialism was "scientific," and that therefore he could foresee the future. Capitalism, he prophesied, carried in it the seeds of its own destruction. Every capitalist manufacturer must try to undersell his competitors, and so would install machinery to take the place of workers who must be paid wages. Wages would decrease. People would be thrown out of work. Thus, although more goods were being produced by more efficient methods fewer people could buy them. As each manufacturer fought for his narrowing market, he would substitute more and more equipment for the labor of human beings and thus reduce his own markets still further. In the end, said Marx, capitalism would so decrease the number of buyers of its goods that it would have to find new markets abroad. But there the process would continue, and eventually capitalism would destroy itself when its markets were exhausted. It would then be replaced by "socialism" meaning government ownership and control of the economy.

Marx and his fellow worker Engels did not say what would happen to the dialectical process once "socialism" was achieved. They spoke of the state "withering away" when there was no more private property and when people were therefore wise and good. Toward the end of his life Marx prophesied a distant future called "communism" where each man would contribute according to his ability and receive according to his needs. The outlines of Marx's "communism" were sketchy and his followers have felt free to fill them in as they chose.

The errors of this Marxist thinking are apparent to anyone who looks at the United States with unprejudiced eyes. Capitalism has enormously increased the number of goods available and has also lowered their cost, but wages have increased—not decreased. The most capitalistic country in the world is also the country in which the workers have the highest standard of living.

Moreover, Marx failed to see that the middle class, small in his day, would become the largest class of all. Indeed it includes a very great part of the population in the United States, Canada, and the western European countries. Another striking proof of Marx's errors is the contrast between life in West Germany, which is part of the Free World, and East Germany, which is a Communist state. The largely capitalist system of West Germany has achieved a post-war recovery and prosperity spectacularly greater than the recovery of East Germany under Communism. Indeed, all western Europe, where there is a large measure of modern capitalism, is prosperous. Capitalism in the United States, moreover, provided the Marshall Plan aid which enabled western Europe to rebuild the factories and railroads destroyed in the war.

Because all these facts prove that Marx was wrong, Communist leaders try to deny them, falsify them, or hide them wherever possible. Communist newspapers, films, school textbooks—everything presents a false picture of life in the Free World and particularly in the United States. By jamming Western broadcasts, keeping out non-Communist publications, and by restricting foreign travel, they can prevent most of their people from learning what the facts really are. Marx said the capitalist system would decay before its collapse, and Communist rulers try to make the "facts" fit the theory!

According to Marx, the power and wealth of capitalists would increase, but their number would grow smaller and smaller as the stronger destroyed the weaker. Meanwhile everyone else would be absorbed into one working class of underpaid, underfed, and powerless human beings. Eventually all society would consist of just two classes, a handful of exploiters at the top, a mass of wage slaves at the bottom. Then the time would arrive when the proletariat or working class would throw off its shackles, seize control of government and all business from the capitalists, and bring in utopia, called by Marx "the kingdom of freedom." Early in their career, in 1848, Marx and Engels had written the *Communist Manifesto*—a flaming summons to the proletariat to proclaim the world revolution. Its closing sentences are still the most dramatic expression of revolutionary Marxism:

"The Communists openly declare that their purpose can be achieved only by the forcible overthrow of the whole existing social order. Proletarians have nothing to lose but their chains. They have a world to win. Proletarians of all lands, unite!"

Revolution or Reform?

In the course of the generation after Marx's death, his ideas spread to many parts of the world. In each country the people who accepted Marx's view of life combined it with the ideas and experiences they already had; thus, there came to be several different types of Marxism. In Russia, where the Czars had absolute power and the people had little freedom of any kind, Lenin and other followers of Marx became convinced that improvement could come about only through violent revolution. Other Marxists who believed in revolution turned to Lenin and the Bolsheviks—later called Communists—as leaders.

But in western Europe, many people who were impressed by some of Marx's thinking did not agree with him that a proletarian revolution was necessary or desirable. While they too realized the many evils in the capitalist system of that period, they believed that these evils were already being gradually remedied, partly by the united action of the workers in trade unions, partly by laws, partly by the capitalists themselves. These more moderate reformers argued that gradual change was more desirable and more lasting than a total revolution. They agreed with Marx that the government should own and operate certain important basic activities like transportation, banking, coal mining, and so on, but they also believed that many economic activities should be left in private hands.

Today the Socialist parties in western Europe are among the most determined opponents of Communism. Communists consider them dangerous enemies first, because they represent the working classes which the Communist want to organize for themselves; second, because they have supported the political freedoms which the Communists must destroy to obtain unchallenged power. In countries such as East Germany or Poland which Communists have taken over from within, one of the first steps has been the planned destruction of the Socialist parties and leaders.

As Americans See Marx

Marx's ideas have become the foundation of the thinking of millions of people. Every child in a Communist country must learn and accept them. Every action taken by Communist leaders must be justified as true Marxism. It is essential that Americans examine them critically. Because our education teaches us to collect all the facts *before* forming theories, most of us would quickly conclude that Marx, who never understood America or our system of competition and free enterprise, could not be an accurate prophet or a sound guide. The position of working men, far from becoming weaker, has grown stronger through the trade unions and because of more enlightened management. In fact, in England the Labor Party governed the country from 1945 to 1951.

In the United States and the other free countries there are countless small businesses, so that thousands of people are in what Marx called the capitalist class. Marx was wrong when he predicted that the capitalist class would grow smaller. The ownership of business and industry, which Marx thought would be concentrated in a very few hands, has spread out to millions of people who own insurance policies, a few shares of stock, or pension rights. Those evils and injustices which Marx observed in the mid-nineteenth century have largely disappeared. As an American sees it, the very bases of Marx's call to revolution simply do not exist.

But in many parts of the world this is not the case. In countries which have just won their independence and have little or no industry, ownership and management of the country's resources are often concentrated in a few hands. People in such countries, ignorant of how the American enterprise system actually works, have no facts or experience by which to criticize Marx's ideas and prophecies. On the contrary they find them attractive, since Marx promises to the underdogs who revolt all the power and privilege now held by their more fortunate fellows.

What is "Capitalism"?

Because of the difference between our experience and that of these underdeveloped countries, the word "capitalism" has come to have different meanings for us and for them. To us it means opportunity, competition, a complex pattern of society in which wages, prices, and profits shift constantly depending on the interplay of unions, consumers, managers, owners and government.

In many parts of the world, however, "capitalism" means the control of the principal business and industry for the benefit of a few. It is not surprising that the Communists use the word "capitalism," with its ugly meaning in some parts of the world, to try to arouse distrust and hostility toward the United States. Because of this, some well-informed people have suggested that the word "enterprise" would better describe the type of economic system which we have in the United States.

What Influences Human Beings?

Americans do not agree with Marx about the character of human beings. Most Americans are strongly influenced by the teachings of the great religions that all men are capable of both good and evil. We see human beings as individuals, each one formed by his particular parents, early surroundings, education, which combine to form him into a unique person. Because he has experienced many different influences he is capable of many different actions, and no one can accurately predict what any one person will do on all occasions. Marx on the other hand claims that the all-important influence is a man's class; if you know what class he belongs to, you can predict just how he will act. For instance, the Soviet rulers claim that because Americans are "capitalists" they will always try to oppress the rest of the world!

That wealth and selfishness often go together has been observed from earliest times; religious teachers who never heard of Marx have stressed it again and again. Therefore, Americans should not be surprised if a grain of truth be magnified into a mountain of envious condemnation which of course is just what Marx's theory does. And the richest country in the world dares not forget how easily the envy of its poorer neighbors can be changed into hatred, as in the case of Cuba, when their desire for progress and their ignorance of facts makes them susceptible to Marxist propagandists.

The Use of Force

On using force to change the world, most Americans would disagree sharply with Marx. Most of us believe that changes which are forced upon unwilling people by superior power cause as many evils as they remedy. Force is a last resort, only to be used when all means of persuasion and argument have failed, and even then only in cases where people's lives and security are obviously threatened. To Marx and Engels, however, force was a necessary part of revolution. Marx had little patience with reformers, humanitarians, "improvers of the condition of the working class," who, he thought, were trying to oppose the onrush of the inevitable revolution. His writings urge the overthrow of existing society by force rather than its peaceful change through law.

But the most telling argument against Marxism is the Communist states which claim to be founded upon it. In the Soviet Union, Communist China, in Hungary, Poland, and East Germany, in North Korea, Cuba and the other satellites, Marx's "kingdom of freedom" is a totalitarian state where the many are ruled by the few. Millions of people have lost their property, their liberty and even their lives in the name of Marxist promises. Yet there are other millions who do not understand what Marxism has become. These people are targets for Communist propaganda. If we want to help them keep their freedom, to choose something better than Marxism, we must have a clear idea of what has happened to Marxism in the past seventy-five years.

For this understanding we turn to the second great leader of Communism, the strategist of revolution, the Russian Lenin.

LENIN 1870-1924

3

Lenin

There is a saying about France that is also true of Russia: "The more it changes, the more it is the same." Today's Soviet tyranny is the direct descendant of a Czarist tyranny already centuries old when Lenin was born in 1870. Unlike the countries of western Europe and the Americas, where the people had gradually won civil liberties and a share in their governments, Russia in the nineteenth century was still an absolute monarchy. Although the nobility varied in wealth and in the lands they controlled, they were sharply separated from the peasants who were almost slaves.

1181934

Not until 1861 was serfdom, like that in the Middles Ages, abandoned in Russia. Over both nobility and peasants the Czar had the power of life and death. There were no laws or constitution to check his power, and how cruelly he used it depended on the personality and whims of the particular Czar. Secret police, confessions forced under torture, exile in Siberia, and death blotted out the few brave men who demanded reforms.

How did it happen that while the people of western and central Europe were winning more and more freedom from their rulers, Russians lay so long under the crushing heel of the Czars? A thousand years of Russian history gives the answer. Differences between Russia and the rest of Europe go back to the fourth century after Christ, when the Roman Empire divided into Eastern and Western Empires. In the Western Empire, of which Rome was the capital, the language and alphabet were Latin, official Christianity was Roman Catholic, and many independent units of government survived because the Romans permitted more self-government than any other rulers of the ancient world. From the civilization of the Western Empire were formed the nations and civilizations of western and central Europe: Italy, England, France, Spain, Germany, Scandinavia, Poland, Austria, and so on—whence came most of the people who built America.

In the Eastern Empire, of which Constantinople was the capital, the language and alphabet were Greek, official Christianity was Greek Orthodox, and the rule of the emperor was absolute, for, according to Eastern custom, the ruler had absolute power over his subjects. From the civilization of the Eastern Empire came the Russian alphabet, Russian religion, and Russia's absolute system of government.

By contrast with the western world, Russia has suffered great disadvantages. Western Europe has had written languages and well-developed civilizations for three thousand years, whereas written language in Russia is only a thousand years old, dating from the ninth century after Christ when two Christian missionaries from the Eastern Empire used a form of the Greek alphabet to write down the speech of the semi-barbaric Slavic tribes who inhabited what is now Russia. Since all of western and central Europe used the Latin alphabet and all educated Europeans knew Latin, language differences cut Russians off from the stimulating and vigorous life of the rest of Europe for almost a thousand years. They missed the broadening experience of the Crusades, the development of free cities in the Middle Ages, and the interchange of knowledge among scholars who wandered from Rome to Paris, from Brussels to London, from Prague to Vienna.

Russians never felt the desire for religious freedom which gave birth to the many Protestant churches. The Greek Orthodox Church was the only form of Christianity they knew and it was completely under the control of the Czar. Thus it was never a counterbalance to royal power as were the churches of western Europe. Most important of all, the Czar's power over the lives and liberties of his subjects was unlimited. The great mass of the peasants, unable to read and write, were practically the slaves of the landowners, and the landowners in turn had no rights against the Czar. Three hundred years after the English nobles had won important rights for themselves and all Englishmen in the Magna Charta, the Russian Czar, Ivan the Terrible, displayed his power to a visiting Englishman by ordering one of his courtiers to jump to certain death.

In fairness to the Russians, we must remember that for generations their energies were absorbed by endless wars against the Tartar invaders from Asia who swept across the unprotected Russian plains, burning homes and murdering everyone in their path. Eventually the Russians drove out their Tartar conquerors, but not until the latter had strengthened the Russian tendency toward absolute, or as we now say, totalitarian, rule. Later enemies came from the west—Swedes, Germans, and Poles. Russia did not win the seacoast of the Baltic, which meant easy access to the west, until the reign of Peter the Great—1689-1725. His efforts to bring western discoveries and ideas to Russia resulted in new industries and a great new city, St. Petersburg (now Leningrad), but they did not bring individual freedom or checks on the absolute power of the Czar.

The Ice Begins to Crack

The American Revolution in 1776 and the French Revolution of 1789 set off a chain reaction which penetrated even the frozen tyranny of Czarist Russia. The armies of Napoleon, on fire with the French revolutionary cry of "Liberty! Equality! Fraternity!" swept all the way to Moscow and, though driven back defeated, they shook Russia to its foundations and lit the desire for more freedom among the educated class. Russian history in the nineteenth century is a story of the continuing struggle between the increasing number of Russians who wanted to break the chains of ignorance, poverty, and tyranny, and Czars who tried to make the chains even tighter. Violence bred more violence.

The liberal Czar, Alexander II, who freed the serfs in 1861, was assassinated by a group of Russians who were convinced that only by killing their rulers and destroying the whole government could they achieve a better world. These Nihilists (from the Latin word *nihil,* or nothing) had none of our democratic institutions through which to spread their ideas. There was nothing resembling a Congress, all printing was heavily censored, and the secret police were everywhere, often worming their way into the Nihilists' own groups. Other Russians tried the more constructive method of working among the peasants, hoping to arouse them to want more political rights, and serving them as teachers, doctors, and nurses. But the obstacles were enormous. The peasants understood so little of what the reformers were trying to do for them that they sometimes turned them over to the police.

Russian Power Expands

Along with stern control of life within Russia there was pressure outward. Throughout Russian history there had been occasional attacks on neighboring areas, but in the eighteenth century there began an organized expansion led by the Czars themselves. Peter the Great had changed Russia from an inland country to a seapower by pushing her frontiers west to the Baltic Sea. In the east he seized land from Persia to the western and southern shores of the Caspian Sea. His successors in the eighteenth century pushed south to reach the Black Sea. Large parts of Poland and the Ukraine were seized by Russia when Poland was divided up among Prussia, Austria, and Russia. Georgia, the future home of Stalin, and Turkestan came under Russian control. Meanwhile in the Far East, Russian colonizers were settling in key points on the Pacific and staking out claims to parts of Siberia.

The process continued through the nineteenth century, extending Russian domination farther and farther eastward over the half-civilized peoples of central Asia. Russia took the Liaotung Peninsula from Japan in 1895 after Japan had taken it from China. By various deals with the weak Chinese government of the early 1900's, Russia asserted claims to Far Eastern positions which she has maintained ever since. In the west, Finland and Bessarabia came under Russian rule.

The conquest of all these peoples, whose race, language and customs differed from the Russians, created many problems for the Czars and their successors, the Soviet rulers, but created a huge empire also.

Over a hundred years ago the British Minister of Foreign Affairs, Lord Palmerton, wrote:

"The policy and practice of the Russian government have always been to push forward its encroachments as fast and as far as apathy or want of firmness of other governments would allow it to go, but always to stop and retire when it met with decided resistance, and then to wait for the next favorable opportunity to make another spring on its intended victim."

Industry Comes to Russia

Meanwhile, capitalism was developing in Russia. A hundred years after the Industrial Revolution began in western Europe, factories began to be built in Russia, largely financed and managed by British, French and other west European interests. Between 1881 and 1896 the number of factory workers rose from 770,000 to 1,742,000. Contrary to the impression the Communists try to create, Russia was already partly industrialized before the Bolshevik Revolution in 1917 and in certain areas, such as manufacture of artillery, excellently equipped. In these factories labored the working class, the Russian part of the world proletariat which Marx had predicted would overthrow the existing governments.

Marx had not expected Russia to take the lead in class war. Like many Germans, he regarded the Slavic Russians as his inferiors. Moreover, according to his explanation of history, the bourgeoisie would have to establish capitalism before the final revolution would be possible. And in Russia during Marx's lifetime, there was little capitalism because there were few factories—Russia was still in the agricultural Middle Ages. Marx was greatly surprised that his work *Das Kapital* was translated into Russian in 1868, even before it was put into English. Russian reformers, blocked on every side by the Czar's tyranny and the peasants' ignorance, had begun to read Marx.

Lenin's Early Life

Among Marx's eager Russian readers was the young son of a school inspector in the town of Simbirsk on the Volga River. Although not of the nobility, the Ulyanov family was well-educated and, like so many educated Russians in the nineteenth century, seriously interested in bettering the lives of the people. The father wore himself out trying to improve the schools in his district, only to see all his work destroyed in an outburst of Czarist oppression. The oldest son was hanged for his part in a plot to kill the Czar. The second son Vladimir (who is usually known by his revolutionary name of Lenin) found getting an education made difficult by the fate of his brother. Only his mother's persistence finally obtained permission for him to live and study at Kazan, and later at Samara. There he studied Marx and became convinced that Marx's interpretation of history was accurate and that class war was the only way by which Russia could be freed from the evils of Czarism. Lenin had given up the Christianity of his family long before and now his belief in Marx's ideas became the religion of his entire life. But Marx had never explained how the class war was to be fought, what was to be its strategy, who were to be its officers. This was the task to which Lenin set himself.

By this time there were thousands of industrial workers in St. Petersburg (now Leningrad), and a wave of strikes broke out in 1896-7. Lenin and his fellow Marxists distributed revolutionary literature and tried to organize the workers into a revolutionary party. But his activities ended with exile in Siberia in 1897. Czarist exile was much milder than the forced labor imposed by the later Soviet government on its political prisoners, and thus Lenin could write letters, obtain books and magazines, and enjoy the companionship of the fellow-revolutionary Nadya Krupskaya, who became his wife. When he returned to Moscow in 1900, he found the police hot on the trail of the

Social Democrats (as the Russian followers of Marx were called). He decided to continue his revolutionary work from abroad, chiefly from England and Switzerland.

Lenin Plans the Revolution

Marx had failed to say just how the revolution of the proletariat would come about; therefore, Lenin's first problem was to work out a revolutionary program to fit Russia and eventually the world. Russia presented a particularly difficult problem, because the change from a farming to a factory society was only just beginning. The peasants greatly outnumbered the industrial working-class who, according to Marx, would bring about the revolution. Moreover, Lenin realized that neither the peasants nor the working class had enough education to provide the necessary leadership. That would have to come from educated men like himself. Lenin's solution of these difficulties was the Party (now called Communist) which he first outlined in the pamphlet, *What Is To Be Done?*, published in 1902. Here he described the organization of a small, carefully selected, disciplined and secret group of men determined to overthrow the government in power and set up a Marxist state.

Secret organizations had existed in Russia for generations, forced underground by the secret police and press censorship. But these groups, like the one to which Lenin's older brother had belonged, had been loosely knit and thus easily destroyed by the police. Lenin saw the need of a strong central authority exercising absolute discipline over all its members. Each member must obey without question the orders received from above. Only one or two at the top would know all the plans; the members often would have to carry out orders in ignorance of their purpose. This prevented the police from tracking down a whole group after they caught one member, but it made the men at the top very powerful indeed since they were not answerable even to their own associates. This practice of centralized authority was called by Lenin "democratic centralism." It is far removed from our idea of democracy which includes the responsibility of leaders to those they represent.

So began the Party—called Communist after 1917. Now Lenin had united the prophesies of the German Marx with the revolutionary underground of Czarist Russia. As the world has learned to its sorrow, it was a fateful union.

At first there was opposition from Lenin's associates in the revolutionary movement. Many of them believed in freedom in our sense of the word; freedom of speech, freedom of thought, freedom to work with other parties. In this they resembled the Socialists of western Europe. Even in those early days some of these Russian moderates saw where Lenin's autocratic Party would lead. In 1903 it was Trotsky (later to be Lenin's close ally) who wrote:

> "The organization of the Party takes the place of the Party itself; the Central Committee takes the place of the organization; and finally the dictator takes the place of the Central Committee. . . ."

Although Lenin failed to win many of his fellow-revolutionaries to his idea of a secret organization, he succeeded in strengthening his own hold on the Central Committee of the Social Democratic party. An example of his political cleverness occurred at a party convention which had to meet in England for fear of the Russian police. Having on one occasion polled a majority vote for his program, Lenin began to call his faction the Bolsheviks or majority party, from the Russian word for "large." His opponents were named the Mensheviks, or minority party, from the word "small," although as a matter of accuracy the names should have been reversed. In the struggle for control of the Russian Marxists the name Bolshevik was an advantage to Lenin.

The Social Democratic party of Russia at that time was a political party as Americans understand the word. Lenin's Bolshevik Party, however, more closely resembled an organized conspiracy. Because the Communists (as the Bolsheviks came to be called) have continued to call themselves a "party," they have been able to take advantage of the freedom which the United States and other free countries grant to political parties. In actual fact, since the early twentieth century, Communist Parties have not really been political parties at all, but self-chosen, centrally controlled and disciplined organizations for taking and holding power.

The First Revolution—1905

Lenin was in Switzerland when the first Russian revolution took place. Defeat by Japan in 1904 and 1905 set off a spontaneous and nationwide uprising which tried to bring to Russia some of the democratic freedoms of western Europe. Soldiers, sailors, peasants, workers, educated men and women, even some of the nobility took part. For over a year they seemed successful. A Duma (a kind of imitation of our Congress) was called. Censorship of the press was relaxed. Soviets, or councils of workers and peasants, were organized all over the country, and some held considerable power. Then the Czar regained control and most of the reforms were lost. But if the revolution itself was a failure, it had shown the weakness of the Czarist government and had given valuable training to those who would lead the successful revolution of 1917.

Lenin's active part of the 1905 revolution was small, but he wished to learn everything possible from the experience, interpreting it always in the Marxist terms of dialectical materialism and the class struggle. He was more determined than ever to perfect his secret autocratic Party inside or outside the Social Democratic party. When he found that he could not persuade his moderate associates, the Mensheviks, to adopt his program, he used more drastic means to strengthen his power and weaken theirs. While he argued that the members of any revolutionary party should accept orders from above without question, he himself disobeyed party orders whenever he did not agree with them.

Against the wishes of the majority he urged his followers to collect stores of arms, which were paid for sometimes by outright holdups and sometimes by using funds which had been given to his party for peaceful purposes. When the Central Committee called Lenin to account for disobeying orders and using means the majority disapproved of, he frankly admitted that he had purposely carried confusion into the ranks of the Mensheviks who had opposed him and boldly stated that he would always do so in case of a split. In other words he would use any weapons whatsoever, even against those of his own party who disagreed with him.

Here we see clearly the Communist doctrine that the "end justifies the means," a doctrine used to excuse cruelty and treachery on the ground that the "dictatorship of the proletariat" was necessary to bring the Marxist "kingdom of freedom." The Mensheviks, like the Socialists of western Europe, were too humane and freedom-loving to accept such a doctrine and by the time World War I began they and Lenin had definitely parted company. Among the small group of Russians who remained loyal to Lenin was the Georgian, Djugashvili, known later by his underground name of Stalin.

Lenin Guesses Wrong

In the summer of 1914 Lenin watched the war-clouds grow darker over Europe. As a Marxist he saw the approaching war as the death struggle of the capitalistic states. He confidently expected that all the working class parties of Russia and Europe, whether Socialistic, Menshevik, or Bolshevik, would see that the revolutionary moment had arrived and refuse to support the capitalist and bourgeois governments of their various countries. He was terribly shocked when the German Socialists remained loyal to Germany, the French Socialists to France, and so on. When he recovered from the blow, he was more convinced than ever that only a Bolshevik Party dictatorship could bring about the proletarian revolution. For the next three years from Switzerland he attacked the "reactionary war" and called for the "revolutionary war." Beyond the "revolutionary war" he did not look. He realized, of course, that the revolution of the bourgeoisie against feudalism had not yet happened in Russia, and therefore he did not expect the "dictatorship of the working class" could take over society at once. But unlike many other Russian Marxists, Lenin did not propose to wait. The Party would take over. The Party would train the workers, educate the peasants, destroy all the former ruling classes. Although at first it would have to be a dictatorship, this would not last, thought Lenin. When the evils left by capitalist and land-owning classes had been swept away, everyone would be so wise and good, not having any private property to make them bad, that things would almost run themselves, and the state would "wither away."

We know now how wrong Lenin was. The Communist Party did bring about the revolution and did take control of the nation. But the government was always a dictatorship of the Party, not of the working class, and it never showed any signs of withering away.

Lenin Discovers "Imperialism"

In 1916, the last year of his exile in Switzerland, Lenin wrote a book destined to have worldwide influence in this century. The word "imperialism," as used in the Free World (and as used in this book in reference to Russian imperialism) has always meant the occupation and rule of other countries by outside powers against the will of the people themselves. In his book *Imperialism: The Highest Stage Of Capitalism,* Lenin gave the word a totally different meaning.

He observed that banking and industrial interests of the capitalist countries like Great Britain, France and Germany were expanding into new areas in search of raw materials and new markets for their manufactured products. As a convinced Marxist, Lenin saw this expansion as part of the "class struggle"—a sort of international class-war in which the industrialized nations of the West were the "capitalist oppressors" and the not yet industrialized peoples of Asia and Africa were the "toiling-masses." By this view Great Britain, France and Germany were of course "imperialists" because they owned colonies. So also was the United States because although it had almost no colonial possessions it was a capitalist country with investments overseas.

Lenin went even farther. He claimed that World War I, then raging around him, had been caused solely by the rivalry between the "imperialist" countries for overseas markets. This was true according to the Marxist materialistic interpretation of history but it was not true according to the facts. The First World War had come about more because of nationalistic and political conflicts than because of commercial rivalries.

Lenin's definition of "imperialism," like Marx's doctrine of the "class struggle," was an over-simplified and distorted interpretation of very complex facts. But it had great propaganda value, then and later. In 1916 Lenin used the term to explain the persistence of capitalism, which he said, was now in its last "imperialistic" stage. To Lenin this also explained why the living conditions of workers in the capitalist countries had improved instead of worsening, as Marx had predicted they would. The workers, he said, were profiting temporarily by the "imperialist" exploitation of the "toiling masses" overseas. In 1917 the Bolsheviks used the term as an excuse for seizing the factories, mines and banks owned by the British, French and German "imperialists." In 1918 the Bolsheviks gave it as a reason for taking Russia out of what they called an "imperialist" war.

With Lenin's successors, the term "imperialist" has largely replaced "capitalist" as a means of attacking the United States and its allies. As we shall see later, its propaganda value has been enormous.

The Democratic Revolution of March 1917

In March 1917, while Lenin was still in Switzerland, a revolution broke out in Russia. It was not a Marxist revolution. Three years of defeat in World War I had completely destroyed the people's faith in the Czarist government. When the soldiers were ordered to fire on a crowd which had assembled to demand food, they threw down their arms and joined the rebels. The government collapsed. Into the breach stepped, not Lenin's Bolsheviks, but a group of nobles, professors, men of moderate views, who hoped to complete the work of 1905 and transform Russia into a democracy like England, France, or the United States. They formed a Provisional (or temporary) Government. At the same time Soviets (Councils) like those of the 1905 revolution were gradually being formed all over Russia, in the larger cities, in the army, and later in the country areas.

For a time it looked as if the centuries-old tyranny of the Czar had given way peacefully to a democratic republic on the western European model. The Provisional Government set free all political prisoners, abolished all racial and class distinctions; established equal rights for women, trial by jury, freedom of press, organization, and assembly; provided for elections based on universal suffrage, the independence of Poland from Russia, and other democratic achievements. In April, 1917, Lenin called Russia the "freest country in the world." But he had not changed his Marxist plans.

Lenin Makes History to Fit Marx

When the Czar abdicated in March, 1917, Lenin was in Switzerland. He was on fire to go to Russia, but the Provisional Government knew his extreme views and was not anxious to have him return. Moreover, Germany lay between him and Russia, and the two countries were at war.

It was the German government which solved his problem. Knowing of Lenin's opposition to the war, they arranged for his passage in a sealed train across Germany, hoping that when he arrived in Russia, he would weaken the Russians' will to fight and thus aid a German victory. This is just what happened, although the smashing defeat of the German armies by the Allies in 1918 made the German victory over Russia useless.

From the moment of his arrival in Russia in April, Lenin worked to bring about the Marxist class revolution. With the Bolsheviks in Russia and those like Stalin and Trotsky, whose exile had been ended by the Provisional Government, Lenin planned the Bolshevik Revolution. Circumstances helped him. Lenin took advantage of the Provisional Government's delay in carrying out reforms. The Provisional Government really represented the ideas of the upper and middle classes; the Soviets throughout the country represented the demands of the workers and peasants. As time went on, their differences of purpose were harder and harder to resolve. The peasants who had wanted land for centuries now took advantage of conditions to seize it from the landlords without waiting for a constitution or permanent government. The workers began to take over the mines and factories. While the Provisional Government wished to continue the war against Germany, the soldiers simply refused to fight and deserted in thousands. Finally, the non-Russian peoples like the Finns and Ukrainians, who had been brought into the Russian Empire by conquest, demanded complete freedom and separation from Russia. The confusion played into Lenin's hands.

Within a few months Lenin's Bolsheviks had established themselves in key points throughout the capital and had won a large following in the Soviets of soldiers, workers, and peasants. In the fall of 1917 Lenin decided that the time was ripe for the Bolshevik Revolution. He organized the Politbureau of six men to direct the Communist Party in seizing and governing Russia. Although many of his followers still shrank from violence, his determination carried the day, and the Bolshevik (now called the Communist) Party took over control of the government on November 7, 1917. The Communist Party has controlled Russia ever since.

Lenin became the Premier of the first Soviet Government, Trotsky the Commissar of Foreign Affairs, Stalin the Commissar for Nationalities (meaning the non-Russian peoples like the Finns, Georgians and Asiatic peoples of Siberia). The new rulers knew everything about how to make revolutions, nothing about how to run a government. Only one had ever had any business experience. But they had complete faith in Marxism as the explanation for everything; they believed themselves chosen by history to bring about the proletarian revolution in Russia and the world. Convinced as they were of the accuracy of Marx's prophecies, they expected similar revolutions to take place in other parts of Europe almost immediately. They were sure that the "toiling masses of workers" in Germany and other countries would follow their example, overthrow the capitalist governments and unite with Communist Russia to bring a new and better day for all mankind. They believed as strongly in their mission to make a better world as have many Christian missionaries. Indeed to the early leaders of the Russian Revolution Communism was a religious faith, replacing the Greek Orthodox Christianity which they had rejected with scorn.

In the task of governing Russia, the Communist leaders had no intention of cooperating with those whose views differed from their own. Before he seized power, Lenin had insisted on the need for a Constituent Assembly to write a permanent constitution for Russia. Such an assembly was elected by popular vote and met, for one day, in January 1918. When it turned out to have a majority of Mensheviks and moderates, Lenin angrily dissolved it by threat of arms. Thus, the pattern of Communist power was set, permanently. Since that day there has never been an election with truly free choice.

Russia Leaves the War

In spite of desperate appeals from Russia's allies, Great Britain, France and the United States, the Soviet government decided to withdraw from the war as quickly as possible. There was widespread popular opposition to continuing it; moreover Lenin distrusted all capitalist countries. The Soviet leaders signed a humiliating peace treaty with Germany in the spring of 1918. In order to discredit the Czarist government and the so-called "imperialist" governments of western Europe, the Soviets made public all the Czar's secret papers, proclaiming that they would never profit by deals made at the expense of other peoples.

Various peoples which had been unwilling subjects of the Czars were no more eager to be subjects of the Soviets and the revolutionary upheaval gave them a chance to obtain their independence. The Finns had been under Russian domination for a hundred years. Now Finland became a nation. The Esthonians, the Latvians and the Lithuanians, small but distinct nationalities living along the eastern shores of the Baltic Sea, became three separate republics.

The Poles were a special case. Poland had been a great power in the late Middle Ages but in the eighteenth century the country was dismembered by its more powerful neighbors, Russia, Prussia and Austria. The Polish people ruled by these countries never gave up their language, their Roman Catholic religion or their loyalty to Poland as an independent nation. At the end of World War I their dream was accomplished. The republic of Poland was formed in 1918 of areas formerly under German, Austrian and Russian rule.

Government For the People

The destruction of the Constituent Assembly proved that the Communist dictatorship was not to be *by* the people, but it did claim to be *for* the people, that is, for the workers and peasants who were the vast majority. Lenin did not interfere with the peasants' seizure of the landlords' estates. His original Marxist program had called for state ownership of land; however, he understood the peasants' wish to own their own land, and the collective farms were postponed until later. Industry and mines, which had been largely owned by British, French and Germans, were taken over by the Soviet government.

These measures won wide support among the workers and peasants. They even impressed many outside Russia, who thought they saw in the Soviet revolution new and successful means of righting age-old wrongs.

Two Years of Civil War

But revolutions always wear two faces. When great changes take place, many suffer. The men who direct revolutions rarely have pity for their victims lest they be unable to carry out their self-appointed task of changing society for the benefit of another group. Cruelty becomes the other face of revolution.

To the inevitable cruelty of all revolutions, Marxism's teachings of class war added fury. The Reds or Bolsheviks hunted down and murdered the members of the former upper classes. Their opponents, largely former Czarists known as Whites, struck back. Counter-revolutions were assisted by armed forces of British, French, Czechoslovaks, Turks, and Poles, for other countries feared the spread of Red Communism. A small force of Americans and Japanese landed in Siberia. Although they accomplished nothing and withdrew quickly, the Communist government resented our intervention bitterly and has never allowed its people to forget that Americans were their enemies at one moment during the Civil War. It does not remind its people of the generous gifts of food from the United States which saved many Russians from starvation during this Civil War.

In the life and death struggle with the Whites the Communist leaders became more and more totalitarian. Government agents took food from the peasants to feed the towns and the armies and did it so ruthlessly that the peasants began to revolt. Industries were down to a fraction of normal because of the disasters of the Civil War—hunger and inflation. To meet this problem the Government organized "Labour Armies," forcing poeple to work at any tasks the Government needed. A Communist secret police, the Cheka, was organized to deal with counter-revolution, sabotage and, eventually, to suppress any opposition.

The Kronstadt Uprising

The Russian people, who thought the Revolution would bring them better and freer lives, could not accept these methods without protest. In 1921 an anti-Communist uprising took place in the naval base of Kronstadt, one of the chief supports of the 1917 Bolshevik Revolution. Sailors, soldiers, and civilians, many of them Communists, demanded that the Party dictatorship be ended and a more widely representative government put in its place. They protested with words; they were answered with guns. Their defeat was the end of organized resistance to the Communist dictatorship of Russia.

Lenin, however, was alarmed. The uprising persuaded him to modify some of his extreme plans for complete government ownership of all economic activity. Moreover, he needed foreign exchange which he could only obtain through exporting surplus food, and that meant winning the cooperation of the richer peasant farmers, the kulaks. In 1921 Lenin began his New Economic Policy, or N.E.P. as it came to be called, a period which lasted until about 1929. Private business was allowed to operate in small-scale industries and trade, although the government continued to own and operate the principal factories, the railroads and shipping, and controlled all business to some extent. Still there was more freedom for the peasants and for small businessmen than before or since, and many people profited from the opportunity. When the N.E.P. was abandoned after 1929 these people paid a terrible price.

But if Lenin yielded some of his Marxist principles to the needs of the moment, he only tightened the hold which the Communist dictatorship had fastened on the country. The more moderate parties like the Mensheviks which had cooperated with the Bolsheviks in bringing about the Revolution (parties similar to the Socialists of western Europe) were suppressed. So was the possibility of opposition groups within the Communist Party itself. Differences of opinion on matters of policy could no longer be expressed openly by Communists; all had to accept the decisions of the Politbureau. This drastic change from the earlier freedom of discussion to a single dictatorial authority marked a change in the nature of the entire revolution. Theory became less important than practice. The idealist gave way to the administrator.

The Communist International

Of all Lenin's actions which influenced the course of history, the most threatening to us was the founding of the Communist International, the Comintern. Lenin and the other Bolshevik leaders believed that their Russian Revolution would set off similar revolutions throughout Europe. The disorder and misery in Central Europe after the defeat of Germany and the break-up of the Austro-Hungarian Empire seemed ideal conditions for Communist revolutions. Such a revolution did take place in Hungary where a Communist dictatorship ruled for a few months in 1919. The failure of a similar Communist uprising in Germany in the same year convinced Lenin that an international organization of Communist Parties should be formed at once to strengthen and support the world revolutionary movement.

The First Congress of the Comintern was held in the Kremlin in March, 1919. Those who attended were not elected delegates but a varied group of Communists from the Baltic countries (recently Russian, now independent) and war prisoners or Communist sympathizers from foreign countries who happened to be in Russia at the time. Then and later Lenin laid down the rules by which these and other Communists were to promote the "working-class revolution" in their various countries.

He declared that small groups of Communists, known as cells, should be organized and run on the principle of "democratic centralism," that is, rule from the top. Each cell was to exist independently of every other cell to provide protection from the police. Cell members were to obey their superior's orders without question. Cells were to be formed wherever possible, in government offices, factories or universities.

True to their self-appointed position as leaders of the working class, Communists should endeavor to secure control of the trade unions. In Lenin's words:

"A Communist must be prepared to make every sacrifice and, if necessary, even resort to all sorts of schemes and strategems, employ illegitimate methods, conceal the truth, in order to get into the trade unions, stay there, and conduct the revolutionary work within. . . ."

Communist Parties should engage in political activities such as elections and running for office but their principal purpose should be to discredit the political institutions and especially the parliaments of the free countries. The Communists should fight reforms which might improve the conditions of the working-class and so lessen their own revolutionary appeal.

"No parliament can in any circumstances be for Communists an arena of struggle for reforms for betterment of the situation of the working class. . . . The only question can be that of utilizing bourgeois state institutions for their destruction."

The over-riding goal of Communist Parties must be the destruction of the capitalist world:

> "In the end one or the other will triumph—a funeral requiem will be sung either over the Soviet Republic or over world capitalism."

Lenin—Idealist and Politician

Lenin himself seems to have been something of an idealist. No matter how great his power, he was personally modest and informal in his manner in contrast to Stalin who demanded personal adoration from his subjects. Lenin's personality was contradictory; he was a practical politician who knew how to capture and hold absolute power, and an idealist who understood that power corrupts those who hold it, and who hoped that the dictatorship of the working class would give way to a society without classes. As history and psychology teach us, Lenin's hope was impossible, Dictatorships never yield willingly. On the contrary, they must constantly increase their power and destroy opposition for fear they will be destroyed by the enemies their oppression has created.

Lenin's narrow belief in the rightness of the Marxist world revolution led him to reject the deepest wisdom of mankind.

"We, of course, say that we do not believe in God, and that we know perfectly well that the clergy, the landlords, and the bourgeoisie spoke in the name of God in order to pursue their own exploiters' interests. . . . We repudiate all such morality that is taken outside of human class concepts. We say that this is deception, a fraud, which clogs the brains of the workers and peasants in the interest of the landlords and capitalists. We say that our morality is entirely subordinated to the interest of the class struggle of the proletariat. . . . And what is this class struggle? It is—overthrowing the Czar, overthrowing the capitalists, destroying the capitalist class. . . . We subordinate our Communist morality to this task."

"We say: 'Morality is that which serves to destroy the old exploiting society and to unite all the toilers around the proletariat, which is creating a new Communist society.' "

Lenin did not live to see the consequences of his teachings. He died in 1924, after having been greatly weakened by strokes in 1922 and in 1923. During the years of his illness power over the "dictatorship of the proletariat" gradually slipped into the grasping hands of a man who differed from Lenin in background, education, experience and character—the General Secretary of the Communist Party, Joseph Stalin.

STALIN 1879-1953

4

Stalin

In the late eighteenth century the Russian Czars had added to their empire the country of Georgia, a land lying in the Caucasus region between Europe and Asia. Georgia's history had been part of Asia rather than of Europe, and for the three centuries before it came under the Czars Georgia had been under Turkish rule. Even today Georgians consider themselves a separate nationality and they speak their own language, an Asiatic tongue unrelated to Russian which is of the Indo-European family of languages. From this country came Lenin's successor, Joseph Stalin.

There is always difficulty in establishing the facts about the lives of Communist leaders, since "history" can be rewritten or withheld to suit the leadership of the moment. People who occupy columns in one edition of the Soviet Encyclopedia may disappear altogether from a later edition. So may any part of their lives. The "facts" of Stalin's life have undergone several changes. From 1928 on, Soviet writers built up the worship of Stalin by destroying some records and manufacturing others. After his death this process was reversed and in his famous speech to the Twentieth Party Congress of 1956 Khrushchev vigorously denied the accuracy of many Stalinist claims. Our knowledge of Stalin's early life comes from the painstaking researches of historians in the Free World who have dug through this shifting mass of Communist material.

Joseph Vissarionovich Djugashvili, known best by his revolutionary name of Stalin, was born in the small Georgian town of Gori in 1879. His shoemaker father had been born a serf and had been freed in 1861 by the emancipation order of Czar Alexander II; his mother was the daughter of serfs. While the boy was young his father gave up trying to make a living in his own workshop and went to Tiflis, the capital of Georgia, to work in a shoe factory. Stalin could claim later that he came from both the peasants and the industrial working class, although he himself was never one of the "toiling masses" whom he claimed to represent.

The father died when his son was eleven, and from then on his mother supported the family. She had ambitions for Joseph, her only surviving child, although she herself could not read or write Georgian and probably knew no Russian at all. She sent him to the church school in Gori, where he must have felt the class difference between himself and the children from the upper classes, but where he also showed an extraordinary memory and a quick mind. His success was more remarkable because he had to learn the Russian language in which the school was conducted. He always spoke with a Georgian accent.

When he was fifteen he entered the Greek Orthodox Theological Seminary at Tiflis, which his mother hoped would prepare him to be a priest. The teaching at the seminary was dull and dogmatic; the students were treated almost like prisoners, living in barracks and subject to spying by the monks. The Russian heads of the seminary tried to stifle the Georgian patriotism of their students but only succeeded in arousing more anger and opposition. Early in his five years at the seminary Stalin began taking part in antigovernment activities, at first primarily as a Georgian patriot, then later as a Marxist.

Factories had begun to be built in Tiflis and the other cities of the Caucasus while Stalin was still in school, and there was beginning to be a working class. Moreover, Marxists from other parts of Russia were being exiled by the Czar to the Caucasus, bringing with them books, ideas, and contacts with other Russian revolutionaries. By the time Stalin left the seminary in 1898 (authorities do not agree on whether or not he was expelled) he had become aware of Marxist ideas and had joined a Georgian Marxist group. From then on his life follows a pattern almost unknown to Americans, that of the professional revolutionary. He held no regular jobs but got his living from party comrades and party funds. He organized strikes, led demonstrations, helped print propaganda in various cities of the Caucasus. Some of this propaganda was based on Lenin's publication, *Iskra,* (The Spark) which was being smuggled into Russia from abroad and was the center around which an organized revolutionary party was beginning to form.

The police caught up with Stalin in 1902, and from then until January, 1904, he was in prison. He returned to find that the Marxist movement, called the Russian Social Democratic Party, had split into two parts: the Bolsheviks led by Lenin, who wanted a rigidly controlled Party of a few obedient members (the origin of the Communist

Party), and the Mensheviks, who believed in working with everyone who shared their goals and general ideas. It was a split between autocracy and democracy in the development of the Russian revolution. Autocracy and Lenin won. From the moment he understod the issues, Stalin sided with Lenin.

Stalin participated actively in the Russian revolution of 1905, which lasted longer in the Caucasus than in other parts of Russian. After the revolution failed, Stalin remained in Russia concentrating his propaganda efforts on the oil workers of the Caucasus and gradually enlarging his own contacts with Bolsheviks in other parts of Russia. He wrote frequent articles for Lenin's publications, often urging discreetly that the Central Committee of the Bolshevik Party be transferred back to Russia, rather than maintained abroad. Always taking Lenin's side, he gradually came more and more to Lenin's attention. His patience was at last rewarded in 1912 when Lenin named him a member of the Central Committee of the Bolshevik Party. He had just begun publishing his own paper, *Pravda,* in St. Petersburg when the police cracked down. He was banished to Siberia in 1913 and did not return until the outbreak of the Revolution in February, 1917.

Return from Siberia

It was Stalin's good fortune to return to the scene of action before Lenin or the other revolutionary exiles arrived from western Europe and America. Not being well known, however, he wisely contented himself with holding things together until Lenin's return, he himself taking no part in the quarrels over the proper application of Marxist doctrine which split the revolutionary leaders.

After Lenin arrived from Switzerland in his famous sealed train, Stalin supported Lenin in his struggle to swing the Bolsheviks over to his program for a second revolution to set up the dictatorship of the Communist Party. Although he remained inconspicuous among the revolutionary leaders, he carried out many difficult tasks, acting as a leg-man for Lenin. During that summer of 1917 when Lenin was in hiding and Trotsky was in prison, it was Stalin who held the Party together. When they returned in the fall, Stalin withdrew again into the background.

According to what reliable records we have, Stalin remained in the background during the critical days of October and November, when the Bolshevik Party overthrew the Provisional Government of moderates and took over control of

Russia. He supported the Bolshevik Revolution chiefly through anonymous editorials in his paper *Pravda* in which he savagely attacked not just the bourgeoisie but even those of his own revolutionary associates who had favored moderate change rather than armed revolution. "The revolution," he wrote, "is incapable of regretting or burying its dead."

The First Steps on the Ladder

In the new Bolshevik government Stalin was named Commissar of Nationalities, although there had been no such post in the Czarist or Provisional Governments. Stalin started with only a table for an office, but gradually he gathered around him a staff of Georgians, Poles, Ukrainians, Jews, and others.

His first public appearance as Commissar of Nationalities was in November 1917, when he announced to the Finnish Social Democratic Congress that the Bolshevik Government had proclaimed Finland's independence of Russia. Before the Revolution Lenin and Stalin had promised that the various oppressed peoples of the Czarist Russian empire should be free to set up independent governments if they chose. Immediately after the Bolshevik seizure of power they prepared to carry this out, confident that the various nationalities would first carry out their own Bolshevik revolutions and then join the Russian Bolsheviks of their own accord. It soon became clear that this was wishful thinking. The threat of the disruption of Russia, particularly from the Ukrainians, became so great that in less than two months Stalin changed his ideas. He announced that the principle of self-determination did not apply to the bourgeoisie but only to the "toiling masses." In other words, only to those who acknowledged Bolshevik leadership.

The problem of the relationship between the Russians and the various nationalities which still clung to their individual difference, such as the Georgians, the Ukrainians, the Tartars and others, was partly resolved in 1924. According to the Constitution of that year the republics formed by the various nationalities were federated into the Union of Soviet Socialist Republics, the U.S.S.R. In the minds of the citizens of the U.S.S.R. there has always been a clear distinction between the word Russian and the word Soviet. The word "Russian" refers to the Great Russians, who form more than 60 percent of the population and are in the majority in the Party and state, living principally in the Russian Soviet Federated Socialist Republic, the R.S.F.S.R. The word "Soviet" refers to the country as a whole. This distinction is widely ignored in the non-Communist world which incorrectly uses the terms "Russian" and "Soviet" as if they were inter-changeable.

The next great decision in which Stalin participated concerned the war with Germany. Many of the Bolshevik leaders maintained that they would never make peace with the Kaiser, holding out for a peace with the revolutionary Marxist government which they had convinced themselves would appear in Germany. In the same vain hope, Trotsky dragged out his negotiations with the Germans at Brest Litovsk because he thought the German working class was on the point of revolution. Lenin, more realistically, saw that Russia could not continue the war. He was willing to give up the immediate plans for promoting world revolution in order to save the Communist revolution in Russia. Again Stalin sided with Lenin and both gained popularity through this decision.

Stalin's Web Widens

During the Civil War Stalin's principal task was to maintain the supply of food to Moscow. This he did extremely well, revealing his skill as an administrator and organizer. During this period began his rivalry with Trotsky who as leader of the Red Army was second only to Lenin in power. When the Civil War ended in 1920 Stalin, although not yet widely known, held positions of key importance. As Commissar of Nationalities he managed the affairs of all the non-Russian peoples, with many languages, many religions and many stages of civilization. His Commissariat was the medium through which Russian Communism remolded these ancient ways of life and through which these newly-communized areas in turn influenced the development of the Communist Party.

As Commissar of the Workers' and Peasants' Inspectorate, he was in a position to control the entire administration of the Party personnel. The Inspectorate was intended to correct the dishonesty and inefficiency of the civil service. In line with his Marxist dogma, Lenin believed that the essential goodness of the working class would enable teams of workers and peasants to correct this dishonesty and inefficiency simply by inspecting government offices at any time. Actually, of course, this simply became another, and equally inefficient, part of the bureaucracy, with Stalin in a position to watch the whole government closely.

As a member of the Politbureau from its founding just before the Revolution, Stalin had been one of a handful of men who made policy for the entire country. In 1922 he became General Secretary of the Communist Party, a new post established to make the work of the Central Committee of the Party and the Politbureau more efficient. The Politbureau was supposed to decide all questions of policy and the General Secretariat of the Central Committee was supposed to carry out those decisions. Thus Stalin had power in making decisions and even more power in carrying them out.

Lenin Becomes Alarmed

The concentration of power in Stalin's hands had gone on so quietly that not even Lenin had been aware of it. Unlike the other revolutionary leaders, Stalin always stayed in the background, never putting himself in the limelight and always appearing as Lenin's devoted follower. But now even Lenin became alarmed, partly by the power Stalin had acquired, partly by his use of it. Lenin was especially angry over Stalin's treatment of a revolt in his native Georgia. As Commissar of Nationalities, Stalin at first allowed the various races and areas of Russia considerable freedom. Later he took the position that the rule of all peoples should be centralized in Moscow as had been the case under the Czars.

Alarmed by these and other actions of Stalin, Lenin tried to check his power in the Party and in Russia. He attacked him openly in the official newspaper *Pravda.* He even went so far as to add to his will the recommendation that Stalin be removed as General Secretary. "I propose," he wrote, "that the comrades consider the method by which Stalin would be removed from this position and appoint to it another man . . . more patient, more loyal, more polite and more attentive to comrades, less capricious, . . ."

But it was too late. Lenin's first stroke in the spring of 1922 was the beginning of the end. During the next two years he tried from time to time to check Stalin, but in vain. His will was not read to the Party's Central Committee until four months after his death, and by that time no one dared challenge Stalin's power.

The Quarrel with Trotsky

Trotsky had hoped to be Lenin's successor, and he was not one to submit without a struggle. But in the struggle with Stalin he was hopelessly outclassed. Abandoning his former background position, Stalin now managed all the details of Lenin's funeral to give himself the maximum prominence. Trotsky did not even appear.

Then followed a grim struggle within the Politbureau, in which Stalin now sided with one group against Trotsky, now with another. His most effective tactics were to wait until Trotsky or his friends made some statement about Marxism or Bolshevik policy, then rip it to pieces, showing how it was contrary to what Lenin had taught. This was easy to do, because Lenin had himself made contradictory statements. In trying to carry out the Russian Revolution according to Marx's theories of dialectical materialism and the class struggle, Lenin had twisted some of Marx's ideas and ignored others. Trotsky, too, had changed his thinking in the course of his long and conspicuous revolutionary career. It was easy for Stalin to attack Trotsky for not having followed Lenin.

Stalin, on the other hand, could not be attacked in return. He had done little writing or speaking about Marxist theory or its practical application in Russia and what he had done consisted chiefly of violent condemnation of the bourgeoisie and glowing accounts of the "Promised Land" of Socialism (i.e. Marxism).

Even so, Stalin found that he could not fight Trotsky entirely on negative grounds. The several hundred thousand members of the ruling Communist Party were such convinced Marxists that

Stalin had to explain his struggle with Trotsky in Marxist terms. Trotsky had always been closely associated with Communist movements outside of Russia. He was well-educated by broad European standards and had always maintained that the Russian Revolution could only succeed as part of the world-wide revolution of all the working classes. As late as 1924 Stalin had agreed with him on that. He wrote in his pamphlet *The Foundations of Leninism,* ". . . can the final victory of socialism be achieved in one country, without the joint efforts of the proletarians in several advanced countries? No, it cannot." But in the same year he withdrew the first edition of that pamphlet and wrote another. In *Problems of Leninism* he took the opposite view, that the efforts of Russia alone could build "socialism in one country." Now he could oppose Trotsky on theoretical grounds. Stalin's formula turned out to have two advantages: by emphasizing Russia and Russian efforts he mobilized all the patriotic feelings of a people who were largely ignorant of any world but their own, by soft-pedaling the world revolutionary doctrines he lulled into false security many people in other countries who were afraid of the contagion of Russian Communism.

Now that Stalin was armed with a theoretical weapon as well as his power over the personnel and the daily practice of government, Trotsky and his friends gave up the unequal struggle. Some of them confessed their mistakes and asked to be forgiven, a technique of Soviet dictatorship which has since broken thousands of its fellow-Russians and the unfortunate peoples it rules.

Trotsky refused to recant, but his loyalty to the revolution was so strong that he could not openly attack its existing leadership. He resigned as Commissar of War in 1925, was expelled from the Politbureau in 1926, and from Russia in 1929. But he continued to be a powerful figure with the Communist Parties outside Russia. Stalin carried the feud outside Russia, and it raged all through the thirties, driving Trotsky from one place of exile to another but never silencing his denunciations of Stalin. Finally, Trotsky was murdered by a Communist agent in Mexico in 1940 while at work on Stalin's biography.

Achievements of the Revolution

Until he finally drove Trotsky into exile in 1929, Stalin followed closely the policies of government laid down by Lenin. The early revolutionaries had been sincere if ruthless men, who had believed they could build a better world for the toiling masses of Russia. And in those early days it seemed as though they had. Indeed, only when one contrasts the lives of Russian workers and peasants before and after the Revolution, can one understand how the Soviet government could command such loyalty from its people, and even, at first, win the admiration of people from other parts of the world. These changes deserve to be more widely understood by Americans.

The peasants profited most—at first. In the turmoil of the Civil War they simply seized for themselves the land belonging to nobles and officials. Although this was contrary to the Marxist doctrines against private property, Lenin accepted it as inevitable in Russia. Because the peasants were the producers of food, they were able through the twenties to obtain favorable treatment from the government (especially after the New Economic Policy was established). By 1929 there had developed several classes among the peasants; the kulaks who hired other peasants to help them work their successful farms, a middle group who owned and operated their farms without hiring other help, and the poorest peasants who worked on the kulaks' farms. In the 1920s the peasants began to have the benefits of education and some medical care.

In accordance with Marx's doctrine of the proletarian revolution, the industrial workers in the cities became a favored class. Their children had special educational opportunities. They themselves were placed in every kind of important position. They received (and still do) many social welfare benefits; maternity leave, disability compensation, free care in illness, old-age pensions, and opportunities for vacations. Their factories are centers of interesting social activities.

The first Russian revolution of 1917 granted women full equality of opportunity with men. Under the Soviets, this sharing of opportunity has been extended to include a sharing of burdens, so that Soviet women are found in many jobs which in the western world are filled by men.

One of the most impressive revolutionary achievements was in education. In Czarist days this had been the privilege of the upper classes. Now it was available to all. Thousands of enthusiastic Communist teachers taught the peasants how to read and write; high schools and technical schools were built to train the new generation of Soviet youth. Today illiteracy has practically disappeared. An instance told by two Americans who lived in Russia during the 1920's is illuminating. In 1917 in one part of the Caucasus lived a tribe so primitive that it possessed no written alphabet. By 1932 this same area had its own high school. The foundations of the education system which so impressed the non-Communist world in the 1950's was laid in these early years.

In Czarist days thousands of villages never saw a doctor. Now the Soviet government trains medical technicians and health workers in great numbers.

As we have seen, one of the original principles of the Revolution was the equal treatment of all racial groups, including those not belonging to the ruling group of Great Russians. This policy, with which Stalin as Commissar for Nationalities was closely identified, brought great benefits to the non-Russian peoples in the U.S.S.R. The Jews, who had been a persecuted people under the Czars, were for a time accorded the same rights as other groups, a fact which made many Jews throughout the world sympathetic toward the Soviet Union.

American newspaper men and others who visited the Soviet Union during the 1920's tell us that there was lively interest in the arts, literature and science, and constant interchange with western ideas. The ban on differences of opinion within the Party had not yet spread to the entire country. Along with vigorous intellectual activity went a tremendous enthusiasm for the new life the Russians thought they were building. The patriotism which had been roused by the Civil

War produced new factories, government buildings, schools and hospitals. The price of dictatorship by the Communist Party seemed small compared to the enormous improvements over life under the Czars.

The Five-Year Plans

The watershed of the Revolution was the year 1928. Trotsky was out of the government and Stalin's rule was unchallenged. According to Americans who lived in Russia at that time, there occurred in that year the first indications that a change in Russian life had begun. The dictatorship of the Communist Party was extending its power over all phases of life. Other more spectacular events for a time claimed people's attention. The first of the Five-Year Plans had begun. This was the tremendous program for making Russia an industrial nation in a few years.

The obstacles were enormous and would surely have daunted a less determined man than Stalin. Capital was lacking, trained engineers were lacking, skilled workmen were lacking, crucial raw materials were lacking. Somehow the obstacles were overcome, partly by colossal efforts of the self-sacrificing Russian people, partly by the assistance of highly-paid technical men from the

West, partly by the threat of imprisonment and exile for failure. Every factory had its workers who were agents of the secret police. Grumblers never knew when a fellow worker might denounce them. Those who were branded as uncooperative found themselves in gangs of forced labor.

In order to carry out his plans, Stalin had to adopt the practice of the hated capitalists, more pay for more work. This was disguised as "Stakhanovism," named after the miner who supposedly showed how greater efficiency would produce greater results. It increased the pressures on the workers who often resisted with violence, but it increased production also.

Man-Made Famine

One of the methods of manning the new factories was to bring in peasants from the farms. This was possible on a large scale because Stalin had now begun to transform farming also. Earlier in the 1920s Trotsky had argued that the Marxist doctrine of government ownership of all the means of production required that the individual peasant farms should be collectivized and placed under strict government control. Stalin had opposed this. But now a practical problem arose. The small farms which the peasants owned as a result of the breaking-up of estates in the Revolution did not produce enough food for the growing industrial cities. The government could not collect enough food for the factory workers. If the many small farms could be collectivized into fewer large farms, farm machinery could be used to raise more crops.

But the peasants did not want to be collectivized. Stalin therefore chose the quickest and most brutal way. Since it would have been impossible to collectivize all the peasants against their will, he made use of the envy which the poorest peasants felt for their more successful fellow-farmers, the kulaks. The poorest peasants were promised a share in the land and livestock of their more prosperous neighbors when the kulaks' property should be collectivized. With their help the government was able to wipe out the kulaks. Some were murdered resisting, thousands were sent to Siberia, millions died of starvation when their means of livelihood was taken. The kulaks' lands were then organized into large collective farms on which farm machinery could profitably be used, and the factories were lashed into producing more and more tractors for the farms.

Terrible suffering ruled the countryside. The kulaks killed their livestock and burned their buildings rather than turn them over to the government. Figures tell the story. In 1929 Russia had 34 million horses, in 1933 there were 16.6 million. Thirty million cattle were killed out of 66 million and two-thirds of all the sheep and goats. There was famine in Russia's richest farm land.

The opposition was so strong that Stalin finally slowed down the drive for collectivization and made a few concessions to the peasants' desire for something of their own. But to those in Russia and elsewhere who had eyes to see, the true nature of the Stalin dictatorship was now revealed. The Communist rule would not hesitate to sacrifice the lives of its own countrymen to carry out an arbitrary decision, even when the same plans could probably have been accomplished more slowly without wholesale murder. Among those who were sickened by the cruelty was Stalin's second wife, the daughter of a working-man who had befriended Stalin in his underground days. She committed suicide in 1932.

Death to the Opposition!

There were others, particularly in the government and in the Communist Party, who were out of sympathy with such brutal measures. Stalin increasingly feared plots to overthrow his dictatorship. Most of all he feared the older revolutionaries. He had always hated them for their intellectual superiority; now he feared the moral authority they still held with the Party members and the people. He knew they felt he had betrayed Marxism for the sake of his own personal power. He knew that they were disgusted by the oriental pomp and ceremony which he demanded, so different from the modest manner of Lenin. They had no sympathy with the slavish praise of former Czars which the government promoted.

When a close friend in the Politbureau was assassinated in 1935, Stalin began the great purges and trials which terrified Russia and shocked the world. Some of the "old Bolsheviks" were induced to sign unbelievable confessions of disloyalty and treason. Others testified on the stand that they had plotted to assassinate Stalin, restore capitalism, bring in foreign armies, destroy Russian factories and people. Thousands simply disappeared from their homes without a trace. With the exception of a few of Stalin's hand-picked followers, like Molotov, almost every man who had taken a prominent part in the first fifteen years of the Revolution was wiped out. History books were rewritten to omit the parts they had played.

Among the purged were two chiefs of the secret police which had sent thousands to their deaths. As an example of the extent of these purges—of the 139 men who were members of the Party's Central Committee in 1934, 98 were later condemned and executed.

During the French Revolution this type of terror had produced a spontaneous uprising from the people themselves and the dictator had been overthrown. This did not happen in Russia. The Russian people had simply exchanged the dictatorship of the Czar for the dictatorship of the Communist Party, and under neither had they learned how to unite to overthrow a tyrant. This was partly due to the nature of the Bolshevik Revolution itself. In 1917 leadership of the popular discontent had been quickly captured by a group of professional revolutionaries with a definite program. Convinced by their Marxist gospel that their views were right and all others wrong, they rapidly destroyed possible opposition by silencing the parties that differed with them. Because of the backwardness of Russia, there had always been comparatively few men with ability and training for leadership. Possible leadership from the former upper classes was wiped out during the Civil War, and leadership among the revolutionaries was narrowed down to the extreme Communist group led by Lenin. When Stalin destroyed these in turn, an entire generation of the most intelligent and aggressive Russians disappeared.

Another reason why Russia accepted the purges passively was that the great majority of people were directly dependent on the government. Probably millions of the peasants on the collective farms and workers in the factories were not personally touched by the terror. They still saw Stalin as the leader who had given them jobs, schools, hospitals, security. The loyalty which ignorant Russians had once felt toward their Czar and their church was now directed toward Stalin.

Stalinism Triumphant

With all opposition dead or silenced, Stalin felt free to make Russian life and thought the reflection of his personal preferences. The earlier equality among all Communists gave way to heavy emphasis on rank. Stalin and the higher government officials had better homes, better cars, better food. They appeared at public gatherings in uniforms and with ceremonies which divided them sharply from the common people. "Reserved shops" were set up where Communist officials could buy a rich assortment of goods not available to the ordinary citizen.

The earlier internationalism and respect for racial differences gave way to Stalin's insistence on the superiority of all things Russian. Racial groups like the Jews or the Ukrainians who cherished any non-Russian traditions were frowned upon sternly. In 1938 the Russian language began to be a compulsory part of the education of children of non-Russian nationalities.

The lively intellectual life of the early revolution was frozen to suit Stalin's views. Art and music were judged by his preferences. Books and magazines reflected his style. Painters and sculptors, novelists and playwrights were compelled to produce works which conformed to "socialist realism." This is a Communist term attributed to Stalin and defined in the *Large Soviet Encyclopedia* as a "means of reflecting life in art peculiar to socialist society." In practice this has meant paintings, statues, books and plays which glorify Soviet leaders and serve the purposes of "socialist society." Since the purposes are set by the Party and the Party determines whether the artist or writer is serving those purposes, there can be no freedom for the artist or writer as we understand freedom. The stale monotony of Soviet art is the result.

Some aspects of science, such as the study of genetics and psychology, were forced to conform to what Stalin considered to be in the interests of Soviet Communism. But science which contributed to the industrial and military strength of the Soviet Union was actively encouraged and these scientists became a privileged group.

An active campaign against religion, particularly directed toward the young, tried to remove any religious beliefs which still lingered.

Foreign Policy or World Revolution?

Since the 1917 Bolshevik Revolution the relations of the Soviet Union with the rest of the world have been two-edged. In addition to the peaceful methods of diplomacy and the aggressive methods of war the Soviet Union has had another weapon not available to the rest of the world. In the Communist Parties of the world the Soviet leaders have disciplined fifth columns which spy, sabotage, provoke strikes, create confusion and distrust, and hinder essential legislation at the Kremlin's command. Soviet leaders may preach peace with all nations; but the Communist Parties promote world revolution.

During the 1920's Stalin's interest was so concentrated on building "socialism in one country" that he appeared to have lost interest in the Communist program of world revolution. He went so far as to support Chiang Kai-shek against the Chinese Communists in the struggle for control of China. As the above-ground Communist activity which had alarmed Americans and others at the time of the Bolshevik Revolution subsided, so did anxiety and concern over the dangers from Communism. In 1933 the United States established diplomatic relations with the U.S.S.R., and in 1934 the Soviet Union was admitted to the League of Nations.

But the Comintern was very much alive. Although the activity and success of the different Communist Parties varied from country to country, all followed Lenin's instructions for promoting the world revolution. They formed cells in key places. They infiltrated the trade unions. They placed Communists in newspaper offices where they could influence public opinion. To discredit legally elected governments (which Lenin condemned as "bourgeois"), Communists staged riots and promoted strikes. They were especially hostile to the Socialists or Social Democrats—the parties which represented the working class whom the Communists claimed to lead.

In the first few years of the Comintern the various Communist Parties kept some independence of each other and of Moscow. The strongest Communist Parties in the '20s were the Italian, the German, the French and the Chinese. But as Stalin extended his hold over the Communist Party within the Soviet Union, he strengthened his hold on the other Parties as well. This included the American Communist Party, founded in 1919. Although its membership was small, ranging from a high of 80,000 in 1944 to an estimated low of less than 10,000 today, its secrecy and discipline made it dangerous. It was responsible for many labor troubles, and its spies obtained information for the Soviet Union.

One of its most effective techniques was the use of "fronts," the infiltration of non-Communist organizations by Communists trained to use the organization for their own purposes. The "front" technique became a standard weapon in the Communist (and Soviet) arsenal in the early 1930's. The rise of Hitler and his violent hostility to Communism alarmed Stalin. As a means of opposing Hitler's Nazism and Mussolini's Fascism (which had succeeded in driving the Italian Communists underground) Stalin ordered the Communist Parties to change their tactics of opposition to the Social Democrats and join them to form "popular fronts" against Nazism and Fascism.

This uneasy alliance continued into the Spanish Civil War, 1936-1939, when the Soviet Union sent airplanes and munitions to the Loyalists to oppose the Germans and Italians who were fighting on Franco's side. Communists from all over the world went to Spain to join the Loyalists, as did many non-Communist opponents of Fascism also. The ruthlessness and disregard for human beings which characterized Communist behavior in Spain shocked many of these European and American volunteers.

Throughout this period of the '30s Communists from the world Communist Parties came to Moscow for long or short periods, sharing with other Communists their experiences in revolutionary activity and receiving instructions from the Comintern.

Stalin's Deal with Hitler

To most people of the United States and western Europe, the immediate threat of Nazi Germany loomed far larger in the late '30s than the long-standing threat of Communism. At the time of Hitler's rise to power in 1933 the German Communist Party was the strongest Communist Party outside Russia. But Hitler destroyed its power—jailed, executed or drove its leaders into exile abroad, usually to the U.S.S.R. Thus throughout the '30s Hitler claimed to be Europe's protector against Communism.

Stalin, after his failure to check Fascism in the Spanish Civil War, turned to the western democracies in an effort to find allies against Germany. As late as the summer of 1939 British and French diplomats believed that Stalin was honestly negotiating with them for a defensive alliance against Hitler. The West was totally unprepared for the shock of learning in August 1939 that Hitler and Stalin had made a deal not to attack each other.

This released Hitler from fear of attack from the east and within a few weeks his armies had over-run Poland. World War II had begun. The Communist Parties outside Russia, all of which had been opposing Hitler for years, suddenly discovered (at Moscow's orders, of course) that this was an "imperialist" war in which the British and French were "aggressors." This Kremlin-ordered switch opened the eyes of many former sympathizers. French and British Communists, however, tried to hinder the war effort of their own countries.

Russian Imperialism Once More

Stalin made the most of the opportunity Hitler offered him. His first victims were the Poles.

While the Polish army made a gallant but doomed fight against the Nazi armies, the Soviets took over the eastern half of Poland. Hidden from the world's eyes by the clouds of war, they systematically purged all Poles who could provide leadership for their people. Educated men and women, business leaders, priests were seized, thrown into prison or transported to the dreary Soviet Asia where thousands died. Several thousand Polish officers were murdered by the Russians and buried in a mass grave in the Katyn Forest.

But for many Poles the war did not end. Thousands of soldiers and civilians escaped and found their way to France where a Polish Government in Exile and a Polish Army were formed. After the collapse of France they did not surrender but moved to England and continued the struggle. A handful of Poles from the tiny Polish Communist Party went to the Soviet Union, where the Comintern trained them for the eventual take-over of Poland.

As the Czars had done before him, Stalin seized the lands of peoples unable to resist his power. Within a few months after Hitler's attack on Poland Stalin had established Soviet control over the three Baltic Republics, Esthonia, Latvia and Lithuania, beginning with a demand for military bases. As in Poland, the Soviets destroyed the middle and upper classes by taking away their property and jobs, transporting many from their homes to distant parts of the U.S.S.R. Russians and Russian officials then moved into their homes, businesses and jobs. Esthonia, Latvia and Lithuania became nothing more than Soviet provinces.

When the Soviet Union demanded that Finland give up several strategic areas near the Russian border in December 1939, the Finns refused. The Soviet Army attacked Finland and the Finns resisted. For three bitter months Finland held the Red Army at bay until the Finns were finally overcome by sheer weight of numbers. The Soviet Union tore important strategic areas from Finland and part of its industry as well.

The Great Patriotic War

For almost two years Stalin felt secure. He believed that the "imperialist" war was hastening the world revolution and he prepared for it. At the Comintern's secret school in Moscow, Communists from Europe, Asia, Africa and Latin America were trained in the techniques of subversion, revolution and take-over. Seen from Moscow, the future of the Communist Revolution looked bright.

Then without warning Hitler's armies attacked Russia on June 22, 1941 and for over two years the Soviet Union fought for its life. In the first months of the war the Nazi armies rolled eastward, capturing town after town. Many Russians at first welcomed the German armies as liberators from the oppressive Soviet tyranny they had come to hate. This was especially true of the Baltic states and the Ukraine which is the area nearest Poland. A million Russian soldiers surrendered or deserted, and from them a separate army was formed which fought on the German side. But Hitler regarded the Slavs as an inferior race and the Nazi policy of enslaving them turned the people against the Germans. It made Stalin's task of rallying resistance much easier.

Indeed, it was not loyalty to Communism which Stalin called upon to defeat the invaders but loyalty to the home-land. "The Great Patriotic War" drew upon every strength of the Russian past. The anti-religious propaganda was silenced; Stalin permitted the Greek Orthodox Church to function but kept it under strict control through his own people within the church. The triumph of Czarist Russia over Napoleon encouraged the Czar's successors.

Help from the West was a major factor in Soviet resistance. On the day of Hitler's attack,

Britain's Prime Minister Churchill went on the air to announce that Britain would assist the Soviet Union's resistance by every means within its grasp. A few months later, when Pearl Harbor brought the United States into the war, America joined Britain in supplying war materials to the U.S.S.R., a trickle that grew into a flood and became an essential factor in Hitler's eventual defeat. In June 1944 a list of military supplies delivered by the Western Allies to the Soviet Union was published in the Soviet press. The Soviet citizens were astonished to learn that the United States alone by that time had supplied to the U.S.S.R. 6,430 aircraft, 3,734 tanks, 82 torpedo boats and small destroyers, 206,711 vehicles, 22,400,000 rounds of ammunition, 87,900 tons of explosives, 245,000 telephone instruments, 5,500,000 pairs of boots and more than 2 million tons of food.

War-Time Attitudes Toward the Soviets

American attitudes toward the Soviet Union in the war years were characterized by ignorance, confusion, and ill-founded hope. The ignorance was both long-term and short-term. In the years between the wars the American people had been little interested in the rest of the world, an attitude which helped bring about the United States' refusal to join the League of Nations and the Neutrality acts which were supposed to keep the United States out of war. Very few Americans knew anything about Marx's teaching. The danger from Hitler was immediate and over-shadowed the longer range threat of revolutionary Communism.

During the war itself, the demands of the military situation kept people from learning certain disturbing facts about Stalin's behavior toward the United States and Great Britain. In spite of the massive help he received from them he never became a true ally. His demands for a second front, long before it was militarily possible, were unreasonable and insulting. He was suspicious of every Allied move. He never granted to the Allied planes which were bringing supplies to the U.S.S.R. the permission to land on Soviet bases which would have eased the Allies' supply burden and saved British and American lives.

Americans were confused by the behavior of the Communist Parties, for the role of these Parties as an instrument of Soviet policy was only beginning to be understood in the United States. After fighting against any American aid to Britain right up to June 22, 1941 the American Communists reversed themselves overnight and proclaimed that the war was one of "liberation." In Nazi-occupied France the Communists stopped collaborating with the Nazis and joined the underground.

Possibly to deceive his British and American allies, Stalin announced in 1943 that the Comintern had been dissolved. Supposedly this released each Communist Party from dependence on Moscow. Of course it did no such thing, for the Communist Parties continued to follow the Kremlin's line. The Comintern school where Communists from all over the world were trained in revolutionary techniques was disbanded but the teachers and students simply moved into other revolutionary activities. What seemed important to Americans during the war, however, was that the French and Italian Communists were tough disciplined fighters against the Nazis. Later, when they emerged at the war's end with greatly increased power and prestige, able to deliver millions of votes according to Kremlin orders, they appeared in their true light as instruments of Soviet foreign policy.

Inexperience in the politics of power contributed to American hopefulness that Stalin could be counted upon as a partner in the postwar world. However, British Prime Minister Winston Churchill was aware of Russia's imperialist ambitions, whether Czarist or Soviet, and had a clear understanding of the totalitarian Communist system. When in 1943 it appeared that final military victory over the Nazi-Japanese Axis could be hoped for, Churchill began to consider how military decisions taken during the war would affect the post-war settlements.

Roosevelt and his advisors, on the other hand, were preoccupied with immediate military situations. Roosevelt hoped that personal discussions with Stalin, as at Teheran and Yalta, would bring mutually satisfactory decisions. Through the last year of the war the United States government worked enthusiastically for the formation of a world organization to ensure peace after the defeat of Germany and Japan and invited the Soviets to help draw up plans for forming the United Nations.

With Russian armies pursuing the retreating Germans beyond Russia and into eastern Europe in the summer of 1944, the future of millions of people, Poles, Czechs, Hungarians, Rumanians, Bulgarians, Greeks, Yugoslavs, hung in the balance. Would they be free to choose their own forms of government or would the Russians impose Communist dictatorships upon them? Churchill was especially concerned to keep the Soviets from controlling the eastern Mediterranean, an area vital to Britain's line of communications with its colonies in Asia. Roosevelt was not willing to bargain with Stalin over the countries of this area, but Churchill was. In October 1944 he went to Moscow and made Stalin a proposal: Britain would liberate Greece from the Nazis, Russia would liberate Rumania. In Yugoslavia each would recognize the other's interest. Stalin accepted at once. Soviet troops were already in Rumania; British troops sailed from African ports to drive the Nazis out of Greece.

The Fate of Poland

Poland was to be the world's first unmistakable lesson in how Communism can be fastened upon an unwilling people. The British had gone to war in 1939 to protect Poland's independence; the Polish Government in Exile was located in London and the British government felt a particular obligation to insure post-war freedom for the Poles. The Soviets gave warning of their plans for Poland in the summer of 1944 when their armies neared Warsaw. A small group of Moscow-trained Polish Communists appeared, calling themselves the "Committee of National Liberation." Stalin promptly announced that his armies would place under this committee's control any Polish territory liberated from the Germans. The German armies still held Warsaw. Now the Soviet radio and the "Committee of National Liberation" urged the Polish underground in Warsaw, which had survived five years of German occupation, to make an all-out attack on the Germans. Russian guns were indeed within hearing.

But when the poorly armed Polish civilians attacked the German troops in Warsaw, the Russian troops did not move to help them. Russian planes stopped flying. For two months the Poles of Warsaw battled against the entrenched German army. British and American airplanes dropped supplies when they could, but this was not enough because Stalin refused the planes permission to land behind the Russian lines for refueling, forcing them to fly twice as far on each trip. When the Germans had annihilated Polish resistance and destroyed Warsaw and the surviving underground fighters had surrendered, then and no sooner did the Russians resume their advance into Warsaw against the Germans. By early 1945 Russia had occupied all Poland.

At the Yalta Conference in February 1945 Stalin forced Roosevelt and Churchill to accept his seizure of Polish territory and his Communist "Committee of National Liberation" as the basis

Barents Sea
Norwegian Sea
White Sea
RUSSIANS
FINLAND
NORWAY
SWEDEN
RUSSIANS
Leningrad
ESTONIA
Union Of Soviet Socialist Republics
LATVIA
LITHUANIA
Baltic Sea
Moscow
Kazan
WHITE RUSSIANS
RUSSIANS
Berlin
EAST GERMANY
Warsaw
POLAND
Prague
CZECHOSLOVAKIA
UKRAINIANS
Vienna
AUSTRIA
HUNGARY
Budapest
Caspian Sea
Belgrade
YUGOSLAVIA
ROMANIA
GEORGIANS
Black Sea
Tiflis
AZERBAIJAN
ARMENIANS
BULGARIA
ALBANIA
GREECE
TURKEY
Ionian Sea
Soviet Union In 1939
Soviet Union In 1945
Post War Boundary Changes

of Poland's post-war government, although the Communists had never been more than a tiny minority in Poland. His only concessions were that this new government would contain representatives of other Polish parties and that free elections would be held immediately after the end of the war.

No free elections were held. The Communist government which the Soviets set up did at first include representatives of the Socialist and the Peasant parties. But the Socialists were gradually replaced by men obedient to the Communists and control over the police was tightened. Then, when the Communist government felt that it could dictate the outcome, elections were held, in January 1947. The Peasant Party, which unquestionably represented the great majority of the Polish people, received 10 per cent of the announced vote, the government (calling itself the "Democratic Bloc") received 80 per cent.

Thus, Poland was completely controlled by the Polish Communist Party, as the U.S.S.R. was controlled by the Russian Communist Party. But Stalin did not trust Wladislav Gomulka, the General Secretary of the Polish Communist Party. Gomulka was forced to resign his office, demoted from job to lower job, and finally jailed, although he never denied his Communist faith. Then, in order to keep an unshakable grip on Poland, Stalin placed a Russian general in command of the Polish army and made him Poland's Minister of War.

The Tactics of Take-Over

Poland's fate was shared by other countries of eastern Europe which the Russian armies occupied. At Yalta Stalin had joined Roosevelt and Churchill in signing the Declaration on Liberated Europe, promising "that the establishment of order in Europe and the rebuilding of national economic life must be achieved by processes which will enable the liberated peoples to destroy the last vestiges of Nazism and Fascism and to create democratic institutions of their own choice."

To Britain and the United States this meant governments chosen by free elections. But Stalin had other plans. On the heels of the retreating Nazis the Russians swept into Rumania, Bulgaria and Hungary. The Russian armies carried off thousands of able-bodied men to labor camps in the Soviet Union. In the armies' wake came local Communists trained in Moscow to take over their native countries for Communism.

Take-over was in several stages. The first governments set up after the war included men from all political parties, Socialist, Peasant and Conservative as well as Communist. But in each government the Russians saw that a Communist controlled the police. Then with police protection, the handful of Communist leaders who represented only a small minority of the people were able to destroy the other parties by a program of planned riots, press censorship, phony treason trials and political assassinations. When the other parties were finally leaderless and demoralized, the Communists permitted elections—for a single slate of their own choosing, as in the Soviet Union. And finally, as in Poland, native Communists whom Stalin did not trust were replaced by men completely under Moscow's thumb.

Thus, behind a black-out of communications with the rest of the world the Communist governments in Poland, Hungary, Rumania, Bulgaria and Yugoslavia carried out Stalin's orders. As Churchill phrased it in the speech he made in Missouri in the spring of 1946, an Iron Curtain had descended on eastern Europe.

How Germany Became Divided

Who would control and organize defeated, shattered Germany? Months before the war ended tentative plans had been drawn up for three zones of occupation, Russian, British and American. At the war's end the Allied armies actually held more territory than these planned occupation zones and it was the earnest wish of Churchill that these areas of Germany and Czechoslovakia should continue to be held by the West instead of yielded to the Soviet Union. His warnings about Russian imperialism were not heeded, however. American and British armies withdrew from the large part of Germany they had conquered and the Soviets occupied Europe east to the Elbe River.

At the Potsdam Conference in July 1945 Stalin, Churchill and the new American President, Harry S. Truman, worked out detailed plans for the occupation of Germany (the French were later included and assigned a separate zone made up of parts of the British and American zones). They agreed that Germany should be treated as a unit in all political and economic matters during the period of occupation. The Russians never kept this agreement. German Communists were placed in key positions in the Russian zone; the other German parties, of which the strongest was the Socialist Party, were gradually reduced to helplessness and the familiar process of creating a Soviet satellite was under way. The British, American and French zones, on the other hand, began to establish democratic practices and institutions in the western part of Germany.

In economic matters the contrast was just as glaring. While the Russians were taking apart the remaining East German factories and shipping them to Russia, the Americans were trying to restore the ruined economy of western Germany. Vast quantities of American food and goods poured into the western zones. Business was encouraged to revive and expand under private ownership; the German people worked day and night. The western Allies early realized that the country needed a dependable money system, but the Russians refused to cooperate in setting up a dependable money for all Germany. Finally the Allies decided to go ahead in their own zones, laying the foundation for the rebuilding of West Germany as a key country of the Free World.

Determined to keep East Germany part of the Soviet bloc, Stalin and his successors refused to consider the union of the two parts of Germany by any method which would safeguard the liberties of 53 million West Germans. The 16 million East Germans lived in a police state, their churches persecuted, their economy tied to the other Communist satellites, their rulers the mouthpieces of Russian policy. Millions of refugees from the Eastern Zone have fled to West Germany, "voting with their feet" against the Communist tyranny which Russia maintains in power.

By 1949 the Allies had given up hope that the Soviets would permit the Germans a free choice of their own governments. In 1955 they ended their occupation of western Germany, recognized West Germany as a sovereign nation and admitted it to the North Atlantic Treaty Organization (NATO). The so-called "People's Democratic Republic" of East Germany remained a Soviet satellite.

Berlin—The Free World's Outpost

The occupation agreements made before the war's end had stipulated that until the final peace treaty was signed, Berlin, Germany's capital, would be occupied by the military forces of the U.S.S.R., Great Britain and the U. S. (the two latter gave part of their sectors to the French later). When the American and British armies, in conformity with the early occupation agreements, withdrew from thousands of square miles of German territory, the Russians withdrew from the western half of Berlin and the forces of the western Allies took it over. What they got was a few square miles of land and 3 million people, wholly surrounded by Russian-controlled territory. The only land links between West Berlin and the rest of Allied controlled Germany were two highways and two railways, over Russian controlled land. In other words, Berlin's lifeline depended upon Soviet intentions.

Those intentions were soon revealed. In 1948 when the Allies introduced the new money system which was essential to the rebuilding of Germany, the Soviets cut off the roads and highways between West Berlin and West Germany, sure that they could starve the Allied forces and Berlin's people into abandoning their plans. They were wrong. American and British airplanes, hundreds each day, flew into Berlin's mid-city airport with the needed fuel and foodstuffs, keeping the city alive for more than 300 days.

The courage and skill of Allied airmen, the staunch bravery of Berlin's people were too much for the Soviets. In the spring of 1949 they called off their blockade and agreed to honor the decisions of the Allied Kommandatura, the four-power military government. However, just as in their Eastern Zone of Germany, the Soviets refused to permit the people of the Eastern Sector of Berlin to choose their own government. They maintained Russian soldiers near the city to enforce the unpopular commands of the German Communists who governed East Berlin and East Germany.

The bitter hatred which the East Germans themselves felt for their Communist oppressors flamed into violence in June, 1953. The workers in East Berlin and in other East German cities put down their tools and demonstrated against their Communist bosses. Russian tanks reduced these unarmed demonstrators to submission, but their spontaneous popular uprising showed the world that Soviet military power, not German Marxism, controlled East Germany and East Berlin.

No help from the West came to the strikers and the brief fire of mass protest sputtered out. But individual protests go on. Daily some 600 East Germans, especially young people and professional people, cross the line between East and West Berlin on the first lap of their road to freedom. The contrast between West Berlin's liveliness and progress, East Berlin's drabness and oppression shocks everyone who sees it. Small wonder that the Russian rulers have become increasingly irritated by West Berlin's candle of freedom, burning so appealingly in the gloom of Communist East Germany.

The Betrayal of Czechoslovakia

The pattern of Communist take-over in Czechoslovakia was somewhat different and showed the lengths to which Stalin would go to obtain unchallenged Communist control. As the war drew to a close the Czechs hoped to be liberated from the Germans by American troops and they were bitterly disappointed when a policy decision by the United States government permitted the Soviet armies to occupy their capital, Prague. In spite of this, the Czechoslovakia which was reborn after World War II was a fully democratic state with representative government and a free press. Completely free and secret elections were held in 1946 with all parties represented. When 38 per cent of the vote went to the Communists a Communist, Klement Gottwald, became Prime Minister. Several ministries, including the all-important Ministry of the Interior which controlled the police, also went to the Communists.

In 1948 the United States offered to the European countries devastated by the war a four-year program of massive assistance—the Marshall Plan. The offer, which came to $16 billion, was surely the most generous ever made in the world's history. The Soviets turned it down; the Soviet controlled governments of Poland and Yugoslavia turned it down also. Czechoslovakia accepted, along with all the countries of western Europe.

But the Soviets had plans of their own for Czechoslovakia in the empire they were building.

Stalin summoned Czech representatives to the Kremlin and ordered them to withdraw their acceptance of American aid. Before the elections scheduled for that summer could be held Stalin's Deputy Foreign Minister Valerian Zorin (later Soviet delegate to the United Nations) went to Prague and helped Gottwald organize the Communist take-over in February 1948.

Using the police, the Communists in a few days took control of every aspect of Czech life, government, schools, press, industry, placing Communists in every important position. The pro-western Foreign Minister, son of Czechoslovakia's first president, committed suicide (or was murdered); the president resigned and died shortly afterward. The Iron Curtain had fallen on Czechoslovakia.

Yugoslavia Defies Stalin

When Hitler's armies invaded Yugoslavia they captured the principal cities but the people of Yugoslavia continued to resist. There were two principal resistance groups, the Chetniks who were chiefly Serbian nationalists and the Communists under the Moscow-trained Tito. At first the British assisted the Chetniks; then in 1943 they switched their aid to Tito and his Partisans, assuring his victory over the other Yugoslav resistance forces. At the war's end Tito organized Yugoslavia along familiar Communist lines, collectivizing the farms, taking over all private business, silencing all opposition, imposing rigid censorship of speech and press. Russian advisors were present in every phase of Yugoslav life.

But Tito succeeded in preventing the Russian armies from remaining in Yugoslavia and before long he expelled the Russian civilian officials also. He even went so far as to undertake to unite the Communist governments of neighboring countries into a Balkan bloc. This act of independence infuriated Stalin. His Cominform, newly created to control all Communist Parties everywhere, denounced Tito. "I will crook my little finger and he will fall," Stalin was later quoted by his successor Khrushchev as having boasted.

Tito did not fall. The Yugoslav Communist Party and people supported him in his defiance of Stalin. To bring him to terms Stalin cut off credits he had promised for the Yugoslav Five Year Plans. He purged Polish, Hungarian, Rumanian and Bulgarian Communists whom he suspected of wanting to follow Tito's independent course.

When Tito turned to the West for economic assistance, the United States and its allies faced a difficult decision. Should they aid an admittedly

Communist country whose leaders are committed to the destruction of capitalism? Or should they refuse the Yugoslavs and thus discourage the first sign of national independence in the Soviet empire? Their decision to give credits to Yugoslavia was based on the increasing difference between Tito's form of Communism and the Soviet variety, and on his independent foreign policy.

In Yugoslavia, workers' councils have some authority over wages and prices and receive a share of profits. Small private businesses have been re-established. Over two-thirds of the prices are set by the individual enterprise, not by the central government. Peasants' protests have stopped the collectivization of the farms. Contacts with the West are freer and more numerous than in the case of the U.S.S.R. Yugoslavia has been so independent of the Soviets that it was violently attacked for the Communist sin of "revisionism" in the declaration of the 81 Communist Parties issued in December, 1960.

The West Defends Itself

Any hopes of post-war cooperation with the Soviet Union which the American people still cherished were dispelled by Soviet conduct in the United Nations. Far from upholding the purpose of that organization to build a peaceful and stable world, the Soviets used it as a forum for falsehood and hostility particularly against the democratic countries of the West. They destroyed the possibility of building the Security Council into a force for peace by vetoing its actions forty times in the first four years—while the United States never used its veto at all. Plans for rebuilding the war-shattered economies of the world by international cooperation in the United Nations and its agencies were rejected by the Soviets in the belief that continued misery and chaos would serve the purpose of Communist revolution better than stability and prosperity. Nor were they willing to consider seriously the United States plan for the international control of atomic energy, proposed to the United Nations in 1946.

The turning point came in the winter of 1947. A Communist rebellion was exhausting Greece, already devastated by the Nazis and the U.S.S.R. was demanding that Turkey hand over some of its territory. When the British Government informed the United States that it was financially unable to help the legally-elected Greek government fight the Communist rebels as it had been doing for two years, President Truman had two choices; do nothing and see the Soviets gain control of the eastern Mediterranean; aid Greece and Turkey to resist. He chose the latter.

The Truman Doctrine, that "Collapse of free institutions would be disastrous not only for them, but for the world . . ." marks the acknowledgment by the United States that Russian Communism was indeed an enemy. In spite of the "Hate-America" chorus which the Communists raised in Europe, the United States made one more major effort to work with the Soviet Union in restoring the wrecked economies of Europe. Marshall Plan aid was offered to the U.S.S.R. and its satellites at the same time it was offered to western Europe. Stalin rejected it, and when Poland and Czechoslovakia appeared ready to accept, he compelled them to reject it also. Under orders from Moscow, Communists and Communist sympathizers throughout the world attacked the Marshall Plan as an "American trick to re-arm Germany."

In 1948 there was no longer any doubt of the Soviet Union's hostility to all "capitalist" countries, especially the strongest one—the United States. Nor was there any doubt of its determination to promote the Communist revolution wherever possible. The take-over of Poland, Hungary, Rumania, Bulgaria, Albania and Czechoslovakia; the Communization of the Soviet occupation zone of East Germany; the blockade of Berlin; the

Communist rebellion in Greece; the abuse of the United Nations; the rejection of the Marshall Plan, and the huge Soviet armies convinced the countries of the West that they must prepare military defenses against the always possible threat of Soviet aggression.

The North Atlantic Treaty Organization was formed in 1949. Canada, Great Britain, France, Holland, Belgium, Luxemburg, Denmark, Norway, Iceland, Italy and Portugal joined with the United States, pledging to "unite their efforts for collective defense and for the preservation of peace and security" and to consider an armed attack on any of them an attack against all. NATO, later joined by Greece and Turkey, became the central defense against further expansion of Soviet power, already deep into Central Europe, and General Eisenhower became the first Supreme Commander of the combined forces with headquarters in Europe.

True to their primary loyalties to Moscow, the Communist Parties of France and Italy fought violently against the treaty. Then and ever since, the Soviet Union and the Communists of the world have pictured NATO as an "aggressive bloc" of "imperialist" countries. When West Germany joined NATO in 1955 Communist propaganda went all out to charge that NATO was reviving German militarism. Europe's painful memories of the Nazis, the Kremlin hoped, would sow distrust of NATO.

In spite of Communist propaganda, however, the combination of NATO's military defenses and the economic recovery made possible by the Marshall Plan has effectively halted the spread of Communism in Europe. The only Western European countries which still have strong Communist Parties are France, where large numbers of the industrial workers still vote Communist, and Italy, where an unsolved unemployment problem contributes to Communist strength.

Far Eastern Conquests

In Asia the story is different.

When Stalin and Roosevelt met at Yalta in February, 1945 the atomic bomb had not yet been tested and Roosevelt foresaw a long war with Japan after the defeat of Germany. The Soviet Union was not at war with Japan, but, as he was doing in Europe, Stalin intended to have a large hand in determining the settlements after the war between the United States and Japan. He struck a secret bargain with Roosevelt. In return for Russia's entry into the war three months after Germany's surrender, the Soviets would receive the southern part of Sakhalin Island, the Kuriles and Port Arthur, territory which Russia had lost to Japan in the war of 1905.

At about this time the Japanese government approached Stalin to ask help in arranging talks for a negotiated peace with the United States and Great Britain. Stalin kept this secret until after the war, preferring that the war in the Far East should continue until he was in a position to take part in the settlements. Five months later at the time of the Potsdam Conference the Japanese approached Stalin again. Stalin could have brought the war in the Far East to an end without the use of the atomic bomb, but he represented the Japanese position to the Allies and the Allies' position to the Japanese in such a way as to prolong the war.

On August 6, 1945 the first atomic bomb was dropped on Japan, on August 8 the U.S.S.R. declared war, and on August 12 Japan surrendered. Russian troops poured into Manchuria and from there across the border into Korea, part of Japan's empire. The United States hastily drew a line across Korea at the 38th parallel. South of that line American armies would take the Japanese surrender; north of the line the Russians would do so. Although Stalin had agreed at Potsdam that post-war Korea should be governed as one country, he did no such thing. The Russians at once began to make North Korea a Communist police state and ignored the votes in the United Nations calling for the uniting of Korea under a government chosen in free elections. In South Korea, however, free elections were held and the newly chosen government was recognized by the General Assembly of the United Nations.

The problems of South Korea seemed far removed from American concern until the day in June 1950 when the armies of Communist North Korea crossed the 38th parallel in force. The United States hurriedly summoned the Security Council of the United Nations, which voted to resist the aggression (the Russians were boycotting the Council at that time and were not present to give their usual veto). The American General, Douglas MacArthur, was named commander of a United Nations force to resist aggression, a force consisting principally of American troops, though altogether seventeen nations sent soldiers.

It was a bitter and bloody war. The troops of the U. N. force defeated the North Koreans and drove them back to the Yalu River, only to be attacked by hundreds of thousands of Chinese soldiers whom Communist China described as "volunteers."

For a second great center of Communist power had established itself in Asia.

Communism Captures China

China has the oldest continuous civilization of any country in the world. Until the nineteenth century China maintained almost complete isolation from the rest of the world and its civilization developed along lines entirely different from that of western Europe and the United States. At the top was the Emperor, the Son of Heaven—the representative of divinity to his subjects. At the bottom were the peasants, the illiterate farmers who made up more than 80 per cent of the population. Between these extremes were the other 20 per cent who ruled China on behalf of the Emperor—the officials, the merchants, the scholars, the local landlords.

When the emperors were strong there was peace, prosperity and expansion; when the emperors were weak there was disorder, misery and lost territory. In the nineteenth century when the weak Manchu emperors were misruling China, the countries of Russia, Great Britain, France, Germany and Japan demanded various trading privileges. The Chinese had always hated and despised "foreign barbarians" but they had to yield to the more powerful western nations. Whole countries were lost by China—Annam to the French, Burma to the British, Korea to the Japanese, Outer Mongolia to the Russians.

The combination of international humiliation and internal misery brought widespread desire for change. Beginning with the unsuccessful Taiping rebellion in the 1850's, China was rocked by a century of upheavals and revolutions. Its greatest revolutionary leader was Sun Yat Sen, the western-educated Christian Chinese who founded the Kuomintang (National People's Party) in 1905. With the support of merchants (including Chinese overseas), students and officer classes, Sun brought about the overthrow of the Emperor and established the Republic of China in 1911. The Chinese, whose idea of government was to worship and obey the Emperor, were given a president, a parliament and a cabinet like the government of Great Britain.

Without a strong central government recognized by all, China soon fell apart into areas controlled by local war-lords and their private armies. Japan saw an opportunity to increase her own empire at China's expense but her demands were so humiliating that the Chinese people were aroused. Sun's successor as head of the Kuomintang, Chiang Kai-shek, began training a Chinese army to resist the Japanese.

Shortly after the Russian Revolution in 1917, a handful of Chinese were attracted to Communism by the writings of Marx and Lenin. Mao Tse Tung, later to become ruler of Red China, was one of them. His father was a small grain merchant who owned a mill; Mao attended the village school and later a normal school in the capital of his province. While serving as a clerk in the library of Peking University he first learned of Marxism-Leninism. He was still very young when he joined the Communist Party and it was many years before he became one of its leaders. Apparently he owed his rise to power to his patience and persistence, his ability to organize military forces for guerrilla activities, and his understanding of China's peasant problems.

The Chinese Communists received some encouragement from the Soviet Union but Stalin was too much involved in national problems and in his quarrel with Trotsky to give them real help. For a time Chiang Kai-shek, leader of the Kuomintang, cooperated with the Communists, since both groups wished to drive out the Japanese. Then he turned on the Communists and drove them out of South China. Under Mao's leadership they took refuge in remote northern provinces of China where they planned and prepared for an eventual Communist conquest of all China.

In 1931 Japan invaded Manchuria. For the next fourteen years, until Japan's defeat by the Allies in World War II, a large part of China was occupied by the Japanese while the rest of the country was bled white by the war. Chiang's forces were driven far into the interior; the big cities, the ports and the railroads were in Japanese hands. By the time the Allies had conquered Japan and forced its withdrawal from China, the Kuomintang government had lost the confidence of many Chinese because of its corruption and weakness.

All this time the Communists in the north had been fighting guerrilla warfare against the Japanese, training armies, developing propaganda techniques for appealing to the Chinese people, training officials, perfecting their plans for turning China into a Communist state. Their success in improving the lives of the peasants in the areas they controlled misled many observers into thinking them reformers rather than revolutionaries. Japan's defeat was the go ahead signal for the Communist conquest of China. Their conquest of Manchuria and north China was assisted by the Soviet armies which released to them the areas they had occupied after the Japanese surrender. The Chinese Communist armies consistently defeated Chiang Kai-shek, whose generals misused the American money and arms he received, for Chiang had been our ally against Japan. By 1949 the Communist armies under their leader Mao Tse Tung had conquered all mainland China. Chiang with the remainder of his forces took refuge on the former Japanese island of Formosa, now called Taiwan.

In taking over control of all China the Communists followed the program of the Russians after the Bolshevik Revolution but with a surer hand. The overwhelming majority of Chinese were peasants and to win their support the Communists promised to take land from the landlords to give to the individual peasants, a procedure which fooled millions of Chinese and many western observers. Nothing was said about collective farms and for two or three years the peasants were allowed to think the land was their own. The same kind of false reassurance was given to the millions of the Chinese middle class, the merchants and businessmen, who were led to believe that a combination of private and state business would be permitted. They were further deceived by the continued existence of the democratic non-Communist political parties which had no real power but were simply a Communist trick to weaken opposition to the government.

When the crack-down came it out-did Russia in ruthlessness. Within little over a year 90 per cent of all peasant homesteads were swallowed up in collective farms. All businesses were "nationalized," that is, the Communist Party owned and controlled them, setting all wages and prices, deciding to what industries the scarce raw materials should go, deciding how the finished products should be used. Many former owners became employees of the state, thus adding their managerial skills to the strength of Communist China. The peasants, merchants, businessmen or professional people who resisted were purged or subjected to organized pressure.

Brain-washing

Not content to make their people outwardly obedient, the rulers of Communist China were determined to re-make their thinking to conform to the leader's plans for them. Their own term, "brain-washing," is completely descriptive. Any man or woman suspected of questioning the leaders' policies was compelled to appear before a group of associates and "confess" his errors. Part of his "confession" had to include criticism of his parents, because the Communists wished to break up the close bonds of loyalty which had made the Chinese family the stable base of society. The offender was received back into good standing only when he had satisfied his accusers that his ideas now conformed. As there were Communist informers in every city block, every workshop and every farm team, people soon learned not to express any unacceptable opinions.

China's intellectuals were a particular target for this "brain-washing," for the Communists feared their links with the West and their training in objective thinking. In the campaign to remake the intellectuals in 1952 the daughter of one of Peking's great university presidents attacked her father in a public speech:

> "Since you cheat all the people, why shouldn't you be cheating me? Even if the parental love between a father and daughter is true, it is completely insignificant compared with love among the masses. Anyway your love is only deceit. . . ."

For achieving their purposes the Communists use campaigns or "movements," a plan of wholesale propaganda and attacks on a particular group of people. One kind of campaign aims to create support for the government in its everyday duties, such as the "Increase Production and

Thrift Campaign," the "Patriotic Cleanliness and Health Campaign," the "Eliminate Illiteracy Campaign." A second kind of "movement" is designed to wipe out large numbers of people suspected of opposing some government program and to terrify everyone else into obedience. There have been the "Land Reform Movement" to wipe out the landlords; the "Suppression of the Counter-Revolutionaries Movement," a quite unrestrained use of terror; the "Three-Anti" and the "Five-Anti Movements," to attack and demoralize the businessmen and industrialists in the cities; and the "Thought Reform Movement" and the "Anti-Hu Feng Movement" against the intellectuals.

The "Resist-America Aid-Korea Movement" began in October 1950 when the Chinese Communist armies, described by the government as "volunteers" entered the Korean War to aid their "Red brothers" in North Korea. Its object was to arouse hatred of the United States in support of the Chinese armies. Exhibits which claimed to prove "germ warfare" by the Americans were displayed in China's principal cities. American prisoners of war in Korea were subjected to "brainwashing," accompanied by physical and mental harrassment which sometimes enabled their Chinese tormentors to extract "confessions" from them. The "Resist America Movement" gave the

Communists an excuse to drive out Christian missionaries, Protestant and Catholic teachers and preachers, and doctors and nurses, who were influential with the Chinese people because of their service to them.

Mao Tse Tung and the Communist leaders quote Lenin to charge the United States with "imperialism" and "aggression," a word which in Communist usage applies only to the "imperialists." In reality they are using one of tyranny's oldest tricks, frightening their people with warnings of outside enemies in order to make them work more and more for less and less. The United States continues to be Enemy Number One. Our refusal to recognize the People's Republic of China as the legal government of China and our opposition to admitting it to the United Nations keeps the Chinese Communists' hatred at fever pitch.

Learning the Hard Way

With the wisdom of hind-sight it is hard to understand why in the war and post-war period, the United States made so many decisions which assumed that the Soviet government wanted a free and peaceful world. One of the most disastrous decisions was made not just by the government but by the country as a whole—the decision to dissolve the tremendous military establishment which had won the war. Under pressure from the citizens to "bring the boys home," the huge American Army, Navy and Air Force were demobilized at breakneck speed. The Soviets, on the contrary, kept their armed forces intact. Since the Nazi and Japanese military power had been destroyed, the strongest military force in the world was now Communist.

The ever-increasing Communist threat makes it important to analyze why Americans were slow to understand their danger. Wishful thinking misled them. After the war Americans were so eager to return to their peaceful lives that they turned their eyes away from the obvious warnings. Judging the Russian people's relation to their government by their own, and with too little knowledge of the Russian past or present, they felt that the Russian people's unmistakable yearning for peace would influence the Soviet government, in other words, Stalin.

But Americans as a whole did not understand the nature of Communist power over its own people. Knowing only western governments in which power begins at the bottom with citizens who choose their officials for limited periods of time, Americans failed to see that in Communist countries power begins at the top and citizens have no direct check on it whatsoever. Once a man becomes a Communist Party official (and Communist officials compose only a tiny fraction of the population) he is in power for as long as he can please his superiors. The wishes of the people themselves have little influence on their permanent rulers.

In the second place, Americans were slow to realize that Communism's goal has always been world domination. To Lenin and thousands of his followers Communism is a religious faith which the true believer should spread by every means possible, including force if necessary. To Stalin and those Communist for whom Communism was less a religious faith than a means to power, Communism had to spread in order to ensure and increase their own power and privilege. Convinced that only they understood the "scientific" laws of the future, they called their own form of imperialism the "liberation of the toiling masses." What had formerly been naked Russian or Chinese imperialism was masked by Communism as a religion, re-enforced by Communism as a means of control.

By the time of Stalin's death in 1953 Americans had learned much about Communist power and Communist imperialism but they still hoped that

Stalin himself was the chief enemy. For centuries Americans had lived under a government of laws administered by men whose Judeo-Christian upbringing had made them respect the rights and worth of each human being. Individual dictators and tyrants they understood, but they also counted on the opposition to assert itself eventually. When Stalin died, Americans told themselves, his successors would surely be more reasonable men, less aggressive, less ruthless. Only a few well-informed experts warned that Stalin's successor could only emerge from those already in power, a group of men who owed their survival to their skill in outplaying their rivals and their ruthlessness in carrying out the dictator's orders.

NEW LEADERS

5

New Leaders

In the last years of his life Stalin grew more cruel, more suspicious of everyone, even of his closest associates. The brutalities of his police state grew worse and worse. Terror reigned throughout Russia and its empire. Leaders in the Party or the government under Stalin were in a dangerously exposed position. If an ambitious Party official seemed to have too many friends, he aroused Stalin's suspicions and was in danger of being purged. If he tried to remain inconspicuous he was quickly pushed aside by bolder men. Those who survived paid for their power and privileges by living in constant fear of their lives. When Stalin died in March, 1953, an almost audible sigh of relief rose from his immediate followers as well as from the whole terrorized empire.

Because there are no laws in the Soviet dictatorship which provide for an orderly transfer of responsibilities, no one knew who would inherit Stalin's power. The five most powerful rivals were: the Prime Minister of the U.S.S.R. whom Stalin seemed to have favored, Georgi Malenkov; the Chief of the Secret Police since 1939, Lavrenti Beria; the long-time Party worker Nikolai Bulganin; the Foreign Minister and old revolutionary Vyacheslav Molotov; and the Secretary of the Central Committee of the Communist Party, Nikita Khrushchev.

Georgi Malenkov had been a political worker in the Party since 1919, had received a technical education and had been one of a five-man State Defense Committee in charge of industry and transportation during World War II. For his success in building up Soviet industrial plants and maintaining the fierce pace of war-time production he became an alternate on the Politburo in 1941 and a full member in 1946. For ten days after Stalin's death Malenkov held the top post in the government, that of Prime Minister, and the top post in the Communist Party, that of First Secretary of the Central Committee. Then his associates (and rivals) compelled him to give up his Party post to Khrushchev.

Under the new leaders, a new day seemed to have begun. Within three weeks of Stalin's death the leaders announced that thousands of convicts and inmates of concentration camps would be released immediately whatever they had been accused of. This included all pregnant women, mothers of children under ten, boys and girls under eighteen, old people and those sentenced for less than five years. With a few exceptions all other sentences were cut in half. For the first time the Soviet leaders admitted that a police terror had ruled the country. Beria, Chief of the Secret Police, Malenkov and Molotov at first seemed to have inherited Stalin's power. In July, however, Beria was arrested and shot, although his death was not announced for several months. But his death did not mean the end of the labor camps or of the secret police, although their presence became less obvious.

Collective Leadership

In the same summer of 1953 Malenkov announced a highly popular new policy. After years of denying the Soviet people the fruits of their own labors in order to concentrate on heavy industry, the rulers proposed to develop "the light and food industries at the same rate as heavy industry." In other words, to give the ordinary citizen a better standard of living. The Party officials had lived well for years, even during the war.

Another reversal of Stalin's policy had to do with contacts with the West. Before World War II, the Soviet Union's contacts with the West had been profitable. Technical know-how from the more advanced western countries had aided the growth of Soviet industry; selected western visitors had seen show-places and gone back to write enthusiastic accounts of the new Russia. But after the war Stalin slammed the door against any such above-board exchanges. Spying by Communist agents and Soviet diplomats went on, of course, greatly aiding the Soviet drive for nuclear weapons, but other contacts ceased almost entirely.

Under Stalin's successors, some trusted Communists were permitted to visit the United States and the western democracies and some Westerners came to the Soviet Union on carefully supervised visits to carefully selected places. On their return the Soviet visitors gave reports of their trips which confirmed the false picture of the West presented by the Party to its people. For instance, a sentence or so about the high buildings in New York would be followed by a half-hour description of slums and racial discrimination. The Western visitors were taken to model schools, hospitals and factories and often returned to praise what they had seen.

For a brief period from 1953 to 1956 the censorship on writers was somewhat relaxed. A novel by the famous Soviet writer, Ilya Ehrenburg, *The Thaw,* gave its name to the books and poems describing how human beings lived and felt, rather than praising the glories of Stalin and Communism.

More than the death of Stalin lay behind this somewhat changed behavior by the new rulers. The tremendous growth of Russian industry and science made them proud of what they had to show the world. They had produced atomic weapons in 1949; in the summer of 1953 they set off a hydrogen bomb. Now that they could match the United States in the most destructive modern weapons they displayed new confidence.

The Rise of Khrushchev

Malenkov's policies of relaxation and emphasis on consumer goods were not favored by all his associates among the top rulers. Nor did he control the Party apparatus which in turn controlled the government. Nikita Khrushchev, on the other hand, had become First Secretary of the Party, a post which enabled him to place his own followers in key positions and increase his own power. In January, 1955, Malenkov was replaced by Bulganin as Prime Minister; Khrushchev remained First Secretary of the Party. The phrase "collective leadership," used in the early days of Stalin, was used again. Although for a time Bulganin and Khrushchev seemed to share the top post, it soon became clear that Khrushchev was leader of the "collective leadership."

In all countries, including free countries, the character of the leader is highly influential in shaping the country's course. In a Communist state, without elections or other checks from the people, it is decisive. What kind of man, the world asked anxiously, had become ruler of the Soviet empire?

Because of the Communist practice of rewriting "history" to suit the leadership of the moment, no one can tell how Khrushchev's early life will finally be described. He himself has given several versions, all emphasizing that he came of a poor family and had to work hard. His Party record, which is reasonably stable, began when he became secretary of the party-cell in a regiment of Red Guards during the Civil War in the Ukraine. From then on he was a Party "activist," first in the coal mines where he worked, later in the Rabfak, an adult education program for workers where he obtained a secondary education. He held an important Party position in the Ukraine during the brutal collectivization of the farms, where his efficiency won him a transfer to Moscow. During Khrushchev's nine years as an important member of the Moscow apparatus (or Party organization) Stalin purged thousands of loyal Communists. Having satisfied Stalin, Khrushchev was rewarded by being made First Secretary of the Communist Party of the Ukraine in 1938.

In this position he directed the deportation or imprisonment of almost two million Poles when the Soviets seized eastern Poland in 1939. "During the Great Patriotic War of 1941-1945," says the *Large Soviet Encyclopedia,* Vol. 46, 1957, "N. S. Khrushchev was with the Army in the field." When the Germans left the Ukraine, Khrushchev and the secret police crushed the Ukrainians who wanted their independence from Russia. Again there were mass deportations.

By the end of the war Khrushchev had built a large group of followers both in the Ukraine and in Moscow. He returned to Moscow in 1949 as a member of Stalin's inner circle and was in daily contact with the dictator until his death. Long experience in the Party had taught Khrushchev patience, and thus it was not until six months after Stalin's death that he achieved the position which had also been Stalin's spring-board to power, First Secretary of the Central Committee of the Party. Through the internal power struggle which is the essence of Communist Party politics, he finally emerged as Stalin's unchallenged successor in July, 1955.

New Methods

The attitude of the new leaders toward the outside world, as well as within Russia itself, differed greatly from Stalin's. Khrushchev in particular quickly showed that he thoroughly enjoyed travelling abroad and being in the public eye. Knowing how to be agreeable when he chose, he had confidence that his personal diplomacy would strengthen both his own position and that of the U.S.S.R. With Bulganin he visited Marshall Tito, Stalin's Communist enemy, in an attempt to restore good relations between the U.S.S.R. and Yugoslavia. Tito received them cordially but refused to acknowledge the U.S.S.R. as leader and pattern of all Communist states.

Visits by Khrushchev to other countries and by heads of other governments to Moscow soon became a regular part of the world diplomatic scene. Bulganin's and Khrushchev's visit to India and Burma in 1955 flattered the leaders and people of those newly freed countries. It also laid the foundations of an aid program in which Russia gave loans and technical assistance to help these countries industrialize. Khrushchev made a highly publicized trip to Great Britain in 1956 and another to the U.S. in 1959.

In Moscow, Soviet leaders attended parties given by the foreign embassies, including the American Embassy. Delegations of scientists and industrial, agricultural and educational experts were invited to the Soviet Union from the West as well as from Asia and Africa; some Soviet experts were permitted to visit these countries in return, always in groups, however. Soviet musicians and dancers made trips abroad. A Communist Youth Festival was staged in Moscow in 1957 and a second in Vienna in 1959 with guests from all over the world. Beginning in 1958 a small number of Soviet students came to American universities and a group of American students went to the U.S.S.R.

Western broadcasts, however, were effectively jammed and only a carefully controlled trickle of western newspapers and magazines was admitted. In spite of the new contacts, the leaders retained a firm grip on what their people might read and hear.

The non-Communist world, reading the volumes of print written about the new Soviet developments, was hopeful that they had more than surface importance. Eager to believe in a change in Communism's hostility to the West, the Free World hoped that the Soviet leaders might be interested in friendly relations after all. Two or three concrete actions re-enforced this impression, for a time. The Korean War was brought to a close and prisoners exchanged. (14,000 Chinese Communists and 6,000 North Koreans refused to return to their Communist homelands). After ten years of refusing to sign a peace treaty with Austria, the U.S.S.R. finally did so in 1955, making Austria independent and withdrawing the occupying troops of the four powers. For the first time since Potsdam in 1945, the heads of the Big Four nations: President Eisenhower; Prime Minister Anthony Eden of Great Britain; Premier Edgar Faure of France and Khrushchev met at a summit conference in Geneva in 1955.

Millions of words were written and spoken about the new era in East-West relations which the West hoped was dawning. Much hope was placed in the Big Four agreement that Germany should be united, that organized cultural and educational exchanges should be encouraged, and in the frequently repeated statement, that nuclear weapons had made war unthinkable. However, these hopes were short-lived. Almost immediately after the summit conference, the U.S.S.R. withdrew its agreements on Germany. It refused to stop its elaborate and expensive jamming of Western broadcasts, being quite unwilling to give its people any version of anything except that approved by the Party. Worst of all, the world learned shortly after the conference that the Soviets had made an arms deal with Nasser of Egypt. Communist drives might have halted temporarily in Geneva, but they were on the march in the rest of the world.

Stalin De-Throned

Khrushchev could not operate in the secrecy which had always surrounded Stalin, for contacts with the non-Communist world opened glimpses of what was happening within the Kremlin. Moreover, there were now many students of Soviet affairs, skilled at interpreting the twists of phrase in *Pravda,* the promotions and demotions within the Communist Party. In the judgment of these experts the rulers of the U.S.S.R. had split into two factions. One group, which the outside world called the Stalinists, appeared to approve of Stalin's methods and wanted him worshipped as the equal of Lenin. The other group, called the anti-Stalinists, wanted to abandon Stalin's terroristic methods and make life easier for the Russian people. Malenkov had shown himself to be of the anti-Stalinist group; Khrushchev, on the other hand, as late as September 1955 appeared to be of the Stalinist faction.

The Twentieth Congress of the Communist Party of the Soviet Union was held in February 1956. The opening speech by Khrushchev contained no surprises. But at the opening of the Congress each delegate had received a set of eighteen printed documents, including Lenin's last letters and testament in which he cautioned against Stalin's increasing power and proposed his removal from his post as Secretary of the Party. On the night of February 24, 1956 Khruschev himself began the famous speech which tore Stalin from his Communist pedestal. He accused Stalin of having destroyed thousands of loyal party workers and officials through torture, false accusations and manufactured evidence. He described in detail the fate of individual Communists liquidated in the purges of the 1930's, confirming what the free world had already known about Communist "justice." The long dead victims were now declared innocent and "rehabilitated."

Khrushchev further blamed Stalin for the disasters of the first years of war, claiming that he had failed to prepare Russia against the Nazi attack in spite of ample warning. During the war itself, said Khruschev, Stalin's leadership had been weak and often mistaken, although at the same time he had claimed the credit for other men's victories. Stalin was guilty, said Khrushchev, of developing the "cult of personality"—he avoided using the term dictator in order to avoid casting doubt on the principle of dictatorship. Specifically, he said:

> "Comrades, the cult of the individual acquired such monstrous size chiefly because Stalin himself, using all conceivable methods, supported the glorification of his own person."

But if Khrushchev and the Soviet leaders now condemned the dictator whom not long ago they had slavishly praised, it was for his crimes against Communists, not for his more monstrous crimes against humanity. Khrushchev found nothing to criticize in Stalin's collectivization of Russia's farms, a process which had cost millions of peasant lives; nothing to criticize in the tyranny over Poland, Hungary, East Germany and the other satellites; nothing to criticize in the Korean War. As with Lenin and Stalin, so with Khrushchev—whatever strengthened the power of the Communist Party was good; whatever weakened it was bad.

From Khrushchev's statement, "We cannot let this matter get out of the Party, especially not to the press," it seems that the speech was not intended to be publicized. Indeed it never has been published in the official newspaper of the U.S.S.R. But of the nearly eight million Soviet Party members and candidates, 6,000 "leading activists" received printed copies. Outside the Soviet Union the Communist Parties received copies, translated and circulated them among their most trusted members. Although only some 20,000 official copies were printed in the Communist bloc, the speech soon reached the outside world. It was printed in full in the United States and recognized at once as an event of supreme importance. Communist leaders, Khrushchev first of all, had admitted that the man they had held up as a god was a liar, a murderer and a coward. As his associates they had shared his guilt, no matter how they now excused themselves. Could the people ever really trust their leadership again?

If Stalin alive had hurt the Party, as Khrushchev said, the Party makes good use of him dead. His corpse still lies beside Lenin's in Red Square, worshipped daily by hundreds of Soviet citizens who bring to this Communist shrine the reverence and awe they had once brought to their Christian altars.

Revolt in Poland

The shock waves of Khrushchev's secret speech reverberated throughout the satellite nations of Eastern Europe. The post-Stalin thaw had already melted the intellectual ice in Poland and Hungary and to a lesser degree in other Communist countries. Criticism of Communist policies and complaints about miserable living conditions appeared in the press.

Polish history had made the Poles hate and fear the Russians; the same was true of Hungary. The Roman Catholic Church to which most Poles and more than half of the Hungarians were intensely loyal, nurtured a spark of resistance to atheistic Communism. Only the secret police and the threat of Russian force kept in power the Polish and Hungarian Communist governments set up by Stalin.

Khruschev's criticism of Stalin undermined the governments Stalin had created. Four months after the speech Polish locomotive workers in Poznan struck against their Communist rulers, raising the slogans, "Freedom and Bread," Out with the Russians," "Down with Phony Communism." At first the government tried to blame the uprising on British and American agents (a standard Communist technique whenever there is trouble within a Communist country) but they were soon forced to admit that they themselves were to blame for the low wages, poverty and oppression. They turned to Wladislav Gomulka, recently released from prison, as the one Communist who could command the loyalty of the Poles and resist Russian pressure.

Alarmed at the threat of an independent Poland, four top Russian leaders including Khrushchev himself traveled to Warsaw. Although Russian troops and tanks were present in Poland the Poles had the courage to demand that the Soviet general in charge of Poland's army be sent home. The Russians gave in, perhaps fearing widespread revolt. For a happy year or so Poland's citizens enjoyed new freedoms. The secret police were disbanded, censorship of the press was lifted, peasants got their land back from the collective farms, the parliament began to debate policies—not just rubber stamp the Communist decrees, and the Roman Catholic Church ceased being persecuted.

Then censorship was partly re-established, economic and political control under the Communist Party became oppressive again. For Gomulka is a true Communist, committed to nationalization of industries, one-Party government and a controlled press. He is convinced that because of the common border with Russia, and because of the once-German territory which Poland has held since the war, Poland must side with the U.S.S.R. in foreign policy.

Although Poland remains a Communist state it nevertheless has certain advantages not shared by the other Soviet satellites. The Roman Catholic Church is tolerated by the government, though not without harrassments. Western newspapers and magazines can be found on the newsstands of Warsaw. Visitors to Poland are freer to travel and speak with the people. Poland has accepted loans from the United States.

In 1958 the most popular Polish joke ran as follows: Do you know the difference between capitalism and communism? Under capitalism man exploits man. Under communism it is just the reverse.

Uprising in Hungary

Hungary's story is sadder. At the time of Khrushchev's secret speech the most powerful man in Hungary was Matyas Rakosi, a Moscow-trained Hungarian Communist who used Stalin's brutal methods and was greatly hated by the Hungarians. Because he himself was a Stalin-like dictator, Rakosy was so frightened by Khrushchev's speech that he relaxed his police terror in the hope of gaining Hungarian support. But when he admitted having purged other Hungarian leaders wrongfully the outcry against him forced his resignation in June 1956. His successor, another Stalinist, was equally unpopular.

Poland's revolution thrilled the Hungarians. On October 24, 1956 a public demonstration to express sympathy for the Poles turned into demands for a new and truly Hungarian government. The people wanted Imre Nagy, a Communist but a long-time peasant leader who as prime minister in the post-Stalin period had applied Malenkov's policy of improving living standards—and like him had been thrown out of office later.

In Budapest, violence broke out against the Hungarian secret police. Soviet troops and tanks that came to help the police were driven back by citizens with make-shift weapons. The Russian-backed Communist leaders left and Nagy became prime minister. He accepted the demands of the citizens that Soviet troops be withdrawn from Hungary, that free elections should be established, and that Hungary should become neutral, not just part of the Soviet empire.

For four joyful days the Hungarians thought they were free. Then the Soviet troops returned in force to put down the revolt. It took them several weeks of savage fighting before the last resistance was crushed. As if to underscore the falseness of Communism's claims to represent the working-class, it was the workers in the Csepel Island factories who fought longest of all.

Imre Nagy took refuge at the Yugoslav Embassy but was kidnapped by the Russians, imprisoned and executed in 1958. A Hungarian Communist wholly loyal to the Kremlin, Janos Kadar, took control as First Secretary of the Communist Party. The secret police were re-established. Russian troops remained in Hungary.

The Hungarians' brief revolt had results far beyond its immediate failure. During a few days when the frontier remained open almost 200,000 Hungarians (of a population of ten million) left their homeland to take refuge in the freer air of Austria and Yugoslavia. Since then the great majority of these have made homes for themselves throughout the non-Communist world, a constant reminder of Communism's essential tyranny.

Shortly after the Hungarian revolt was crushed, the United Nations appointed five distinguished statesmen to report on Hungarian charges of Soviet aggression. Kadar has never admitted them to Hungary, but the commission has had exhaustive interviews with refugees and has condemned Soviet aggression. Its charges have been made at every United Nations General Assembly meeting since 1956, a repeated warning to the non-Communist world of Soviet contempt for the wishes of the people it rules.

Yugoslavia's defiance of Stalin, Poland's launching its own course, Hungary's uprising all proved that when people have a choice between Communism and patriotism, they choose patriotism. Years of Communist education had left the boys and girls completely unconvinced; it was they who hurled their home-made grenades at the Russian tanks.

Communism Through Communist Eyes

During these uprisings a manuscript was smuggled out of Yugoslavia which gave the first inside picture of the operation of a Communist state—from the top. Many ex-Communists had written of their experiences in the lower levels of various Communist Parties. In *The God That Failed,* Arthur Koestler and five other distinguished writers described their reasons for rejecting Communism. In his *Darkness At Noon* and other books Arthur Koestler made clear to the outside world the cruelty and falsehood which are an inescapable part of Communist tactics. In *Child of the Revolution* the German-born Wolfgang Leonhard describes his youth in the Soviet Union, his training at the Comintern school, his activity as a

Communist organizer and official in defeated Germany. The first ten years of Communist rule in China are described in *Ten Years of Storm* by Chow Ching Wen, a former high official in the government of Communist China who escaped to Hongkong. Soviet bureaucracy and its deadening influence on the individual is the theme of *Not by Bread Alone,* a novel written by the young Russian writer Vladimir Dudintsev during the "thaw." Best known to the outside world, though still unpublished in the U.S.S.R. is *Dr. Zhivago,* the poet Boris Pasternak's story of a Russian doctor who welcomed the Russian Revolution for its promise and experienced bitter disillusionment in its results. The novel was awarded the Nobel Prize for literature in 1958 but Pasternak rejected it rather than be forced to remain in exile from his homeland—the choice which Khrushchev forced upon him as punishment for a book the rulers did not like.

Among these and countless other first-hand pictures of Communism in practice, *The New Class* by the Yugoslavian Milovan Djilas holds a special place, for Djilas wrote his book to apply to *all* Communist countries. As second only to Tito in Yugoslavia, his knowledge of Communist practice was unusually deep and wide. "I have traveled the entire road open to a Communist, from the lowest to the highest rung of the hierarchical ladder," he says in the preface to *The New Class.*

Djilas was born of a poor family in a part of Yugoslavia never wholly conquered by the Turks. He grew up a devout Catholic and says that a humane and enlightened priest gave him his first push toward Communism by firing him against the injustice and misery of the life around him. During World War I he was a radical student leader and in 1932 joined the Communist Party of Yugoslavia. He fought as a Partisan throughout World War II and when Tito established Yugoslavia as a Communist state after the war Djilas was one of his closest advisors. He became Secretary of the party in 1948 and later President of the National Assembly.

Djilas never feared to attack wrong when he saw it. He grew more and more critical of Stalin and Russian policy and helped to bring about Yugoslavia's break with Stalin in 1948. But he did not stop there. As he looked at Communist rule from within he became more and more troubled and he published his criticism in the Party paper. When Tito realized what was going on Djilas was forced to resign his office and was expelled from the Party. He was tried and condemned but given a suspended sentence—not immediately imprisoned. When he refused to be silenced and gave anti-Communist interviews to the Western press he was jailed. The manuscript of *The New Class* reached the United States and was published. His sentence was extended to seven years, but in 1961, after serving only four and a half years, he was released.

Although Djilas says in the Preface to his book, "I have concentrated on a description of contemporary Communism touching upon theory only where necessary," Western readers may wish he had given more concrete illustrations of his generalizations. Nevertheless, the book bears out, point by point, the workings of the Communist system as Western experts had analyzed it. Djilas' criticisms are harsh, reflecting the betrayal of his own idealistic hopes.

The theme of *The New Class* is simple and straightforward: the Communist revolution has produced a new class of exploiters. This new class is composed of a small group within the Communist Party who fill all the top jobs, have first claim on all goods and privileges which are available, and shut out any ideas they do not favor by controlling every means of communication, inside and outside the country. Once the party has attained power its most important goal is to maintain itself in power. It remains in power by its totalitarian control of every aspect of life.

In Djilas own words:

"In contrast to earlier revolutions, the Communist revolution, conducted in the name of doing away with classes, has resulted in the most complete authority of a single new class. Everything else is sham and an illusion."

"With the Communist system . . . the power and the government are identical with the use, enjoyment and disposition of almost all the nation's goods. He who grabs power grabs privileges and indirectly grabs property."

"For a long time the Communist revolution and the Communist system have been concealing their real nature. The emergence of the new class has been concealed under socialist phraseology and more importantly under the new collective forms of property ownership. The so-called socialist ownership is a disguise for the real ownership by the political bureaucracy."

"Contemporary Communism is that type of totalitarianism which consists of three basic factors for controlling the people. The first is power; the second ownership; the third ideology. They are monopolized by the one and only political party, or according to my previous explanation and terminology by a new class."

Of these basic factors for controlling the people, which are, of course, control over the government, control over the economy, and control over men's minds, Djilas condemns most severely Communism's "tyranny over the mind."

"History will pardon Communists for much, establishing that they were forced into many brutal acts because of circumstances and the need to defend their existence. But the stifling of every divergent thought, the exclusive monopoly over thinking for the purpose of defending their personal interests, will nail the Communists to a cross of shame in history."

New Worlds to Conquer

Although weakness had been revealed in the European part of the Communist empire its strength in other parts of the world was growing. After World War II dozens of new nations appeared in Asia and Africa, proud of their new independence and eager to improve the conditions of their people. These countries, ranging in size from India with its 400 million down to Mauretania with only a few hundred thousand, had previously been part of the colonial empires of Great Britain, France, Holland and Belgium. These empires owed much of their rapid growth in the nineteenth century to the Industrial Revolution, which in country after country had brought the factory system and hastened the growth of industry and international trade.

The modern industrial system had its beginnings in Great Britain at the end of the eighteenth century, followed in the early nineteenth century by the United States and western Europe. In Japan and Russia the industrial system began in the last quarter of the nineteenth century; in much of Latin America, in India and in

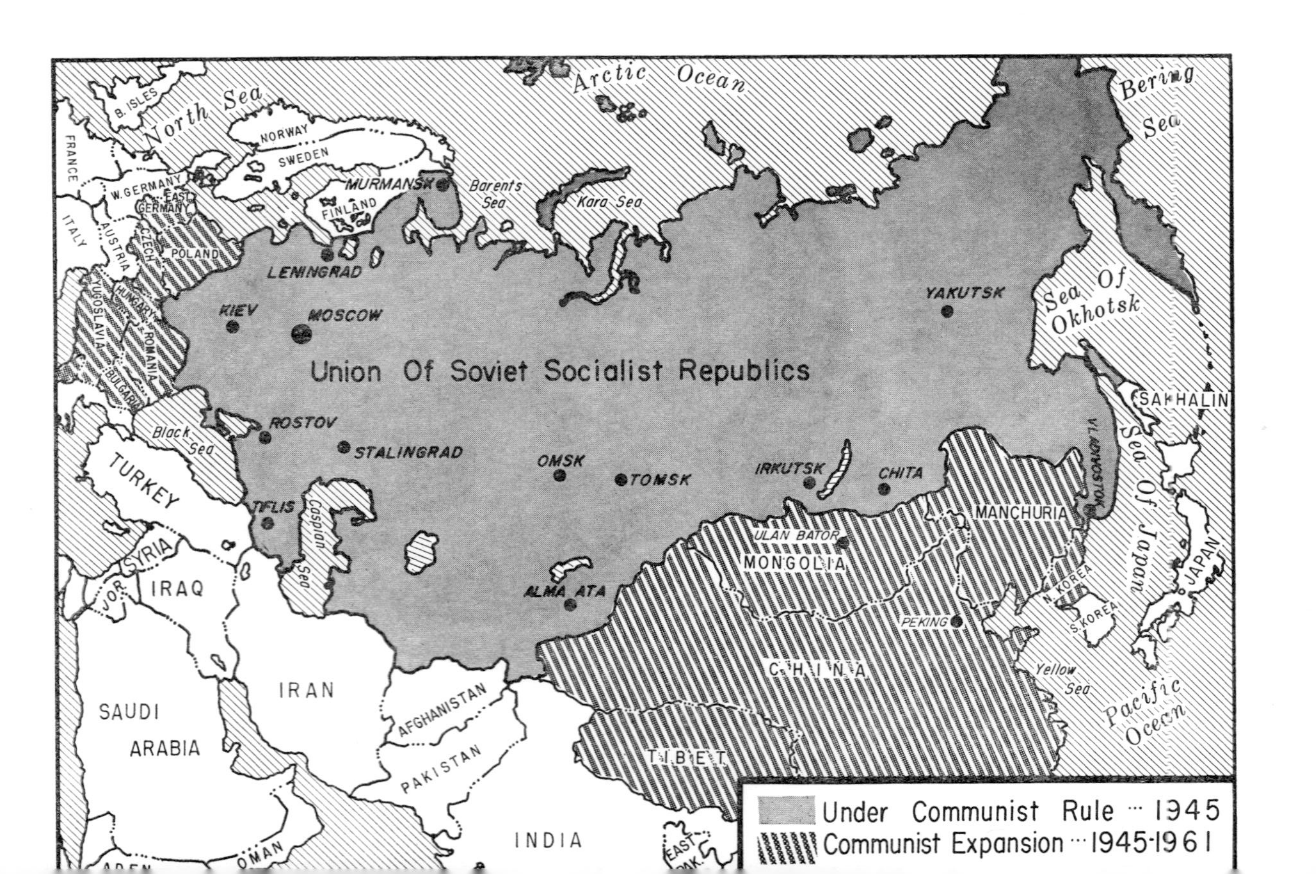
Arctic Ocean
Bering Sea
North Sea
B. ISLES
NORWAY
SWEDEN
FRANCE
W. GERMANY
EAST GERMANY
ITALY
AUSTRIA
CZECH
POLAND
FINLAND
MURMANSK
Barents Sea
Kara Sea
LENINGRAD
YUGOSLAVIA
HUNGARY
ROMANIA
BULGARIA
KIEV
MOSCOW
YAKUTSK
Sea Of Okhotsk
Union Of Soviet Socialist Republics
SAKHALIN
ROSTOV
STALINGRAD
Black Sea
TURKEY
OMSK
TOMSK
IRKUTSK
CHITA
VLADIVOSTOK
Sea Of Japan
TIFLIS
Caspian Sea
MANCHURIA
ULAN BATOR
MONGOLIA
SYRIA
JOR.
IRAQ
ALMA ATA
N. KOREA
S. KOREA
JAPAN
PEKING
CHINA
Yellow Sea
IRAN
SAUDI ARABIA
AFGHANISTAN
PAKISTAN
TIBET
Pacific Ocean
INDIA
OMAN
EAST PAK.
Under Communist Rule ··· 1945
Communist Expansion ··· 1945-1961

China it began in the second quarter of the twentieth. In many parts of the world—including most of the new countries—it has scarcely begun at all. They see in industry and in the science and technology which have accompanied it, remedies for their present backwardness and poverty and they are determined to obtain them.

In the nineteenth century a great gap separated the industrialized nations from the rest of the world. As the nations of western Europe built new industries they found they needed dependable sources of raw materials for their factories and markets in which to sell their manufactured products. Finding in Asia and in Africa both the raw materials and the possible markets, the highly industrialized nations obtained control of many parts of these continents and governed them as colonies. India, Burma, Ceylon and many parts of Africa were British colonies; North Africa and Indo-China were French; the islands of southeast Asia were Dutch; the Congo was Belgian. Germany obtained a number of colonies in Africa but lost them in World War I.

Some colonial powers, Great Britain and France in particular, brought not only stable government but education and modern health practices to benefit the people of their colonies. In many colonies, Great Britain actively encouraged training in self-government along democratic lines. But the spread of education made the colonial peoples aware of and resentful of their inferior positions. Native leaders demanded independence from outside rule. In Asia and Africa this was complicated and embittered by racial differences. The rulers were white-skinned, the ruled were yellow, brown or black-skinned. A hundred times a day an Asian or African in his own country was made to feel inferior to a European, a foreigner. These feelings of resentment against white rulers went so deep that they outlasted the widespread grants of independence after World War II. Bitter memories of the days of "colonialism" formed ready-made tools of anti-Western propaganda waiting for Communist hands.

"Imperialism" and "Colonialism"

The Leninist definition of "imperialism" is a propaganda weapon against the United States as well as against its allies, the so-called "colonial" powers. According to this definition, investments by American businesses in countries overseas are "imperialist exploitation" of the "oppressed peoples" of the world. This propaganda is especially effective in Latin America, where some people feel that certain American business interests have made large profits at their countries' expense, paying the native workers very little and exporting the country's raw materials abroad. Although most of the practices criticized have ceased, unpleasant memories still linger. Communist agitators in many parts of Latin America find it easy to stir up hostility to the "Yanquis."

In Asia and Africa the Communists have an effective weapon against the United States. The well-known inferior position of Negroes in the American South helps Communist propaganda picture the United States to the non-white world as just another "colonial" power. Every picture of white Americans jeering at Negro students in Little Rock or New Orleans is reproduced in millions of copies of Communist publications distributed over Asia and Africa.

"Colonialism" and "imperialism" are vague words which arouse strong emotions in many people. As such they are valuable Communist devices for blackening the United States in the eyes of the world. By calling themselves opponents of "colonialism" and "imperialism" the Soviet leaders present themselves as friends of the new countries.

The December 1960 declaration of the eighty-one Communist Parties attacked the United States and its allies as "colonialist" and "imperialist," and described themselves as "the most active champions of national independence." The truth is that the United States and its allies have freely granted independence to hundreds of millions of people—the Communists have enslaved hundreds of millions.

Winning Friends

The Communist world has a carefully planned and generously supported program to win friends for itself. Each year the U.S.S.R. spends well over one billion dollars for propaganda purposes, employing hundreds of thousands of full-time workers. Propaganda by Communist Parties abroad and through sympathizers in the non-Communist world has gone on since Lenin's day.

Stalin's successors have been tireless and imaginative in presenting the Soviet Union appealingly to the less developed countries. Soviet university students, who must study what they are assigned, have been intensively trained in the languages, customs and ambitions of the people Communism hopes to win. These Asia and Africa specialists are available when opportunity presents itself; Soviet technical experts on Africa were sent to Patrice Lumumba the moment his Congolese Republic was established in June 1960; when

Madagascar became independent in 1960 the only delegate who gave his congratulations in the native tongue was from the U.S.S.R. Soviet newspapers, which print what the Party wishes, publish complimentary stories about the countries being wooed; these then are reprinted in the countries themselves where the people read them with pleasure and pride. The natural result is a favorable attitude toward the Soviet Union.

Scholarships are granted to students from Asia and Africa for study in the U.S.S.R. Khrushchev announced in Indonesia, February 1960, that the U.S.S.R. was establishing a "University of Friendship of the Peoples" for Asians, Africans and Latin Americans, to train engineers, agricultural experts and so on. The Soviet Union poses as being tolerant of all races in contrast with the United States which is charged with racial discrimination as a national policy! Actually there is discrimination in the Soviet Union as between the Great Russians and the non-Russian peoples, and a government policy of discrimination against the Jews.

At the Moscow Youth Festival in 1957, Asian and African delegates were housed two to a room, British and Americans in groups of five. The Soviets have understood, often better than the Free World, the eagerness of the newly independent peoples for recognition and honor, an eagerness which is all the greater because of the economic difficulties they face.

Influencing People

Words alone, whether praising Communism or political freedom, will not build factories or feed the hungry. The leaders of the new countries know that some parts of the world have overcome poverty; they are determined to develop the industrial and economic strength to do the same.

Since World War II the United States and other free countries, individually and through United Nations agencies such as the World Health Organization, the Food and Agriculture Organization, have helped under-developed countries attack their age-old scourges of hunger and disease. Their aid has included loans for industrialization, irrigation projects, agricultural improvement, public health programs. The U. S. government has saved millions of lives through its gifts of food. In addition to government aid, private organizations and independent institutions of the Free World, such as foundations, churches and schools, have shared their personnel and know-how with less privileged countries. The United States government alone gave grants and credits for economic aid amounting to almost $39 billion in the period from July 1, 1945 to December 31, 1957.

Not until 1954 did the U.S.S.R. launch its own aid program. Beginning with an $11 million loan to Afghanistan in that year, Soviet aid has risen to one billion dollars in 1960. Soviet aid has been largely concentrated on a few countries which the Soviets regard as politically and strategically important. Among these are India, the countries of the Middle East, Cuba, and Guinea, a former French African colony in which Communist technicians and Communist aid are trying to show how quickly Communism can industrialize an African country. In India the Soviets built a steel mill which began producing in 1959 and Indian technicians went to Moscow to learn how to run it. Oil technologists from Communist Rumania helped Indians locate oil. Plants to manufacture drugs and heavy machinery were promised to India. Burma was promised a technological institute.

Long term loans with low interest rates are given by the Communist bloc to pay for new industries. As of January 1, 1961, $180 million such credits had been given to Iraq, $195 million to Syria and $500 million to Egypt. This means that Soviet technicians, equipment, and materials have enormous influence in the economic development of these countries. The U.S.S.R. has the contract to build the first two stages of the giant Aswan Dam in Egypt, a project to last years which Nasser hopes will expand Egyptian agriculture and industry.

To some countries such as Cuba, the United Arab Republic and some new African countries, the Soviets supply arms. Their huge armaments industry is constantly producing new weapons which make the older ones out-of-date, and these older weapons can be traded for things the Soviets want. In turn, countries with Soviet arms become increasingly dependent on the Soviets for repair and replacements.

The Communist catch-word "aid without strings" misleads the countries which receive the aid and the West. "Strings" are attached to both Communist and Free World assistance but they are of different kinds because the purposes are different. The Free World tries to make its aid do the most good for human beings and favors projects such as malaria control or the improvement of agriculture. The Communists offer show projects with popular appeal such as street-paving in Kabul, Afghanistan, a stadium in Jakarta, Indonesia, or a hospital in Cambodia which requires Soviet technicians to operate. Whereas the

Free World tries to make its aid serve the people and insists that the receiving governments so use it, the Soviets usually simply announce a credit and let the local governments decide how to spend it. The "strings" are political, as Guevara, Cuba's Communist economic dictator, publicly stated on his return from Moscow.

Soviet foreign trade is government trade and fits the same pattern. It is not for profit, as are the independent enterprises of the Free World, but is planned to promote Soviet purposes. Since Soviet trade is on a government-to-government basis, the Communists believe that it promotes government controlled economies on the Communist model in the newly developing countries. Surpluses of Egypt's cotton, Ghana's cocoa, Brazil's coffee, Cuba's sugar, Uruguay's wool or Bolivia's tin are attractive opportunities for Soviet traders to establish a foot-hold in the economic life of these countries. Local Communists in the receiving country give Soviet aid and trade offers maximum publicity, often over-shadowing the much larger aid and trade of the Free World.

The Communist aid and trade offers do not come solely from the U.S.S.R. but from the entire Communist bloc. In the Soviet bloc each country must concentrate on those raw materials or manufactured products which will strengthen the

Communist program—not on what its people want to buy and use. Surplus products and technicians in these industries are thus available to be sent overseas to those underdeveloped countries which the Party leadership has chosen as targets for Communist influence. In the single month of November 1960, Poland reported news of trade or technical exchanges with the United Arab Republic (Syria and Egypt), Tunisia, Morocco, Senegal, Ghana, and Guinea; Czechoslovakia with the United Arab Republic, Cuba, Iraq, Liberia, Afghanistan and Ghana; Rumania with Togoland and Somaliland in Africa and with India; Bulgaria with the United Arab Republic. Hungary received leaders of student delegations from Cuba, Venezuela, Brazil, Argentina, Chile, Puerto Rico, Liberia, Sierra Leone and West Africa to study Hungarian higher education.

Communist China as Ally

In its efforts toward the newly emerging countries, the U.S.S.R. has had in Communist China a powerful ally. China's leadership has always been ambitious for China to be recognized as the leader of all Asia and as a major power factor in the world. For this they needed heavy industry, a large army with modern weapons, trained scientists and technicians. Their greatest resource was their 630 million people whom they bombarded day and night with radio and printed propaganda to hate the United States "imperialists" and to work ever harder to destroy them.

Their capital resources were very small. From the U.S.S.R. they obtained some loans—not gifts. They forcibly took whatever capital investments were owned by private citizens and they denied their people basic necessities in order to export food and manufactured goods to obtain foreign exchange. When the Korean War ended in July 1953, the Communist leaders launched their first Five-Year Plan, an ambitious program to make China a powerful industrial nation in the shortest possible time.

To attain their goals China's Communist rulers have treated their people so harshly that even Khrushchev became dismayed. For thousands of years the basis of Chinese society had been the family. Loyalty to the family group headed by the father was the one great loyalty—loyalty to the ruler only a pale reflection of loyalty to the family. Many changes have taken place in the family system in recent years, particularly in the freeing of women. Mao and his five million Communists have undertaken to break up family loyalties so that the Chinese people will be loyal only to the Communist state.

In the cities the workers are forced to spend all their time either at work or attending political meetings, marching in parades, or hearing lectures on Mao and Marx. They have neither leisure nor rest at home. In the countryside it is even grimmer. Within about 18 months during 1958-1959 the rulers, not satisfied with the output of the collective farms, herded the peasants into communes. Each of these is a semi-military unit, the size of an entire county. Party officials direct each section of manpower (as they regard human beings) to get the maximum work from them. A husband works in one brigade, his wife in another. Children are kept in nurseries, kindergartens or schools; old people are sent to separate institutions where they also work under supervision. All meals are eaten in the commune's barracks. The sacred ancestral burial grounds are plowed over. The family's past is destroyed, its present torn apart, its future in the shape of its children turned over to the state.

It is hard for Americans to understand any government which cares so little for the happiness and welfare of its own human beings. Movies of the communes, occasionally available to the West, suggest to the viewer that they are nothing more than human ant-hills. But Americans must remember that the belief in the worth of each human being is taken for granted in the United States—but not in China! Traditions of Greek thought, Roman justice, Judaeo-Christian religious ethics have influenced the thinking of all Europeans and Americans, Russians included. None of these influences reached China until a century ago when they were brought by the (often hated) "foreign devils." Policies that no western people could imagine or endure seem to be accepted by the Chinese.

Yet there have been protests. For a brief period in 1957, China's Communist rulers relaxed their iron grip and permitted, even urged people to say what they thought. This period was introduced by an ancient Chinese saying, "Let a hundred flowers bloom together, let a hundred schools of thought contend" and was known as the "Bloom and Contend Movement." But when the "hundred schools of thought" turned out to be highly critical of Communist policies and practice the leadership clamped down hard. Those who had dared to speak honestly were demoted or jailed. Many disappeared. Since then Communist Party rule has been harsher than ever.

Judged in terms of their own goals of industrializing China, Mao and his group have been most successful. Industrial progress is difficult to measure because of different circumstances and different yardsticks. American experts often use the annual growth of a country's gross national product (called GNP for short and meaning everything that is bought and paid for in a single year) as a measure of a country's industrial strength. Growth rates in some periods of industrialization are higher than in others and comparisons are very difficult. However, western students of Chinese figures, making allowance for Communist boasting, believe that China's GNP rose during the years 1953-1957 at an average yearly rate of 7 to 8 per cent. By contrast, the other great—and non-Communist—Asian country, India, raised its GNP at a 4 per cent rate in the 1951-1956 period.

But the agricultural picture remains dark. Whether because of such natural disasters as floods or because of the misery and apathy of the communized peasants, harvests have been disappointing. In 1961 China was forced to buy large quantities of grain from Australia and Canada. However, reports indicate that some harsh practices in the communes have been relaxed in the interests of more production.

Communist China's achievements have underscored the Soviet argument to the underdeveloped countries that Communism offers a quick route to industrialization. Thus, China's industrial success story has become effective Communist propaganda—especially in Asia. Other Asian countries can see in China the industries they want so badly themselves, though not all Asians want to pay the human cost China's leaders have wrung from their people.

Communist China as Rival

Just as the U.S.S.R. is both Communist and Russian, so China is both Communist and Chinese. Sometimes their plans coincide—sometimes one seems to out-distance the other as leader among Communist countries and Communist parties. In the struggle to win southeast Asia to Communism, China has an advantage over the Russians. From the Philippines to the borders of India live millions of Chinese who years ago left China to seek their fortunes. Very often they have made fortunes in their new homes in Thailand, Burma, Malaya, Indonesia, Laos, Cambodia, Viet Nam and the Philippines. They are an important and prosperous part of their new surroundings. Often they are more hard-working and ambitious than their easy-going neighbors and so are resented by them.

After Communism conquered the mainland of China these overseas Chinese were torn between loyalty for the older China represented by Chiang Kai-shek and the Nationalist Chinese on Formosa, and loyalty to Communist China on the mainland. Communist China used every device to win their loyalty, partly to draw on this large source of outside capital, partly as a fifth column for Communist subversion. Communist Chinese in Malaya, for instance, carried on guerrilla warfare for twelve years, first against the British, then after Malaya received its independence, against their own new country Malaya. In 1960, however, it appeared that the attraction of the overseas Chinese to Communist China had been lessened by the ruthlessness of the communes and the aggression in Tibet.

China's second great advantage over Russia in its bid to lead Asians and Africans to Communism is that the Chinese are yellow and not white-skinned, as are most Russians. The resentment which Asians and Africans feel toward all white people is not felt toward the Chinese. Nor are they associated with the "colonial" powers which so recently ruled Africa. The trade and cultural delegations which China sends to Africa, the Africans invited to China on expense-paid tours, the broadcasts to African lands in which Peking viciously attacks the "imperialists," are all Chinese contributions to Communism in Africa.

In its propaganda toward the largely agricultural countries of Latin America and Africa, Communist China claims that its experience of using the peasants as the revolutionary base is better adapted to existing conditions than the "dictatorship of the proletariat" which was set up in Russia.

In its efforts to acquire leadership in Asia, China poses as favoring "peaceful coexistence." At the Bandung Conference of 1955 the twenty-nine Asian and African nations present—Russia was not invited—were eager to believe that Chinese intentions were peaceful, in spite of the Korean War, the Communist guerrilla wars in Malaya and Indo-China, and the large Chinese standing armies. A few years later, however, Chinese Communist terror in Tibet and the flight of the Dalai Lama from his native land, followed by the seizure of Indian territory in the north, aroused fear and doubt of China's "peaceful" policies among many in these same nations.

In 1960 and 1961 there was intense speculation in the Free World about rivalry between the U.S.S.R. and Communist China. On the surface the disagreement seemed about two different views of Marxism-Leninism; Khrushchev and the

Soviets maintaining that Communism would win the world without war, Mao and the Chinese insisting that war between Communism and the "imperialists" was inevitable. Certainly many factors are involved in the disagreement. The Soviet's greater familiarity with nuclear weapons makes them fear large-scale war. The Chinese leaders, on the other hand, feel they need the threat of war to justify their harsh exploitation of their people.

But these are, after all, differences over means —not over ends. Their goals and their doctrine are the same. As the leaders of world communism proclaimed in December, 1960:

> "Communists throughout the world are united by the great doctrine of Marxism-Leninism and by a joint struggle for its realization. The interests of the Communist movement require solidarity in adherence by every Communist party to the estimates and conclusions concerning the common tasks in the struggle against imperialism. . . ."

"Peaceful Coexistence"

The greatest obstacles to Communism's plan of world domination are those countries of western Europe and the Americas which have both the determination to keep their independence and the military and economic power to defend themselves and others against Communist aggression. These nations, usually called the West, of which the strongest is the United States, have so far had the military power to deny Communist aggression a cheap victory and the economic power to offer the world an alternative to Communism.

The Communist leaders know this well. In their declaration of December 1960, they claimed "that United States imperialism is the chief bulkwark of world reaction and an international gendarme, that it has become an enemy of the peoples of the whole world."

"As long as imperialism exists there will be soil for wars of aggression."

But they go on to say that they prefer "peaceful coexistence" with their enemies.

"In a world divided into two systems, the only correct and reasonable principle of international relations is the principle of peaceful coexistence of states with different social systems advanced by Lenin. . . ."

As we read farther we find what the Communist leaders mean by "peaceful coexistence."

"The coexistence of states with different social systems is a form of class struggle between socialism and capitalism. . . . In conditions of peaceful coexistence favorable opportunities are provided for the development of the class struggle in the capitalist countries and the national-liberation movement of the peoples of the colonial and dependent countries."

How is this "class struggle" to be developed?

The Soviet Union is an economic giant, whose satellites contribute to its strength. On the industrial base which Czarist Russia had attained before the Revolution, the Soviet leaders have built the world's second most powerful industrial national, capable of manufacturing the most intricate computers and the most powerful rocket-launching engines. The Communist bloc is centrally controlled, its industries, mines and agriculture fitted into a single plan instead of divided by competition as are the businesses and countries of the Free World. Wages are set by the government rather than by free bargaining between unions and employers. So are prices, and the government decides what people may buy and what will not be available at all. In the Free World each individual may decide how he spends his earnings and as a result increased production means a better standard of living for all.

This centrally controlled economy is a powerful weapon with which to hurt the Free World. The Soviets have suddenly dumped tin on the world market at prices so low that it has hurt not just the companies that sell tin but the countries that produce it, like Malaya and Bolivia. They have encouraged Cuba to take over American businesses without paying for them, then bought Cuban sugar at prices lower than Cuba received from the United States. They have obtained a large share of the oil market in Italy and are in a position to influence Italian policies by threatening to stop the delivery of oil. As they extend credits or make trade agreements with the newly developing countries, they hope to replace the Western business which formerly supplied them. Currently they are offering to Western businesses attractive offers to obtain the technical know-how which they can then use to out-sell these same Western firms.

The Threat of Nuclear War

The Communist leaders declare that "the unprecedented destructive power of modern means of warfare demands that the main actions of the anti-war and peace-loving forces be directed towards preventing war." The world must hope that they mean this, but the record since World War II is not reassuring. From the moment when the atomic bombs were dropped on Japan in 1945 the American and British scientists warned that a new dimension of warfare had opened.

Nuclear knowledge is science and does not recognize national boundaries; any nation with the will and the resources can eventually possess nuclear weapons. Control must be international control or it is meaningless. Immediately after the war and before the hydrogen bomb was developed, the United States proposed to the United Nations a plan to have all nuclear development placed under international control, offering to surrender its own stock-piles and share its knowledge. Stalin refused, being more interested in arming Communism than in protecting the world from nuclear warfare. Continuous efforts by the West to place these weapons under international control were continuously blocked by the Soviets who exploded their first atomic bomb in 1949 and a hydrogen bomb in 1953.

No responsible American or Western statesman could throw away the defenses of his own people without ironclad proof that his declared enemies were doing the same. Where nuclear weapons are concerned, only inspection can supply that proof, or even a small part of it. Soviet delegates use the United Nations for speeches about total disarmament, they demobilize soldiers they no longer need, they talk and talk at endless conferences.

But in the summer of 1961, the problem of an inspection system which satisfies both sides remains unsolved. Meanwhile the number of nuclear weapons grows as more countries obtain them. Great Britain and France have developed their own. When Communist China has atomic weapons, which experts expect soon, the danger will be great indeed, for Communist Chinese leaders have said that if "imperialism" will not surrender peacefully, Communism must destroy it by war.

In addition to economic warfare and the growing threat of nuclear stock-piles, the Free World is subjected to a carefully planned psychological attack. One might almost call it "brain-washing" on a world-wide scale, and indeed the techniques used on individuals are now being used on whole peoples. By promising "peace" on one day and threatening war on the next, Khrushchev and the other Communist leaders hope to confuse the Free World to the point of helplessness. The press of the Free World, which reports everything, can be used to weaken the will of its own people. So can the West's ethical and religious convictions, which have taught us to look for the fault in ourselves. Our free press and our self-criticism are things which strengthen us in the long run, but may be used against us if we are not determined and alert.

Cuba—A Case History

The establishment of a pro-Communist dictatorship in Cuba in the years between 1958 and 1961 opened American eyes to what Khrushchev means by "peaceful coexistence." It was an object lesson in Communist tactics and a warning that certain conditions common to many Latin American countries play into Communist hands. Among these are extremes of wealth and poverty accompanied by rising national pride.

Cuba's closeness to the United States made it inevitable that the United States would be a principal market for Cuba's chief crop, sugar, and that American business would invest heavily in Cuba—a situation which irritated many Cubans whose patriotism was offended by what they felt was their country's economic dependence on the United States.

Cuba's economic and social system was a fertile field for Communist propaganda. Largely based on the sugar produced on vast plantations, Cuba's wealth was in the hands of a few landowners while the great majority of Cubans lived in poverty. The distress of the poor was increased by the so-called "dead season" of unemployment between the grinding period and the new harvest. Marx's doctrine of the "capitalist exploiters" of the "toiling masses" seemed to fit Cuba. Lenin's doctrine of "imperialism" as consisting of investments by capitalist countries seemed to fit the United States. The Communist slogan of "land for the landless" appealed to the peasants' hunger to own their land.

Politically Cuba owed its independence to the United States, having been freed from Spanish rule in 1895 and granted its independence seven years later. The United States retained the right to intervene to restore order, but gave this up in 1934. The free political institutions set up by Cuba's Constitution demanded more education among the masses and more civic responsibility in the upper classes than Cuba had developed under Spanish rule. As a result, Cuba's government alternated between military dictatorships and reform administrations which became as oppressive and corrupt as those they replaced. By the early 1930's there were Cuban Communists in cells organized according to Lenin's instructions.

From 1934 to 1958 the most powerful man in Cuba was Fulgencio Batista, an army officer who was the power behind the president and who was president himself from 1940 to 1944. He ran for president again in 1952 but when he saw that the votes were going against him he took over the army and the presidency and for the next six years ruled as a military dictator. In the first years of his power, the country was prosperous and wages rose. But as time went on Batista's rule became more and more brutal and a growing number of Cubans opposed his police-run state.

Among the opposition was Fidel Castro, a well-educated young man of good family who made his first unsuccessful attempt at revolution in July 1953. His second attempt was organized in Mexico in 1956 and with a handful of followers he landed in the mountainous eastern tip of Cuba where he established a guerrilla army. In the next two years money and followers came to strengthen Castro's forces. Some of the money came from Communist sources, and a few of the followers were Communists, including the Argentine-born Communist Ernesto Guevara, and Fidel's brother, Raul. But the bulk of Castro's support came from loyal democratic Cubans who were fed up with Batista.

For many years the Cuban Communists had passively supported Batista. In the middle of 1958, however, realizing that Batista's days were probably numbered, the top leadership of Cuban Communists decided to switch their support from Batista to Castro. This was of course the familiar Communist tactic of joining a reform group in order to win popular approval and also to be in a position to seize control later. When revolution broke out in Havana and Batista fled, various anti-Batista groups, including the Communists, came together to create a new government, with Castro as head of the nation's armed forces. Throughout the world, including the United States, the revolution was welcomed as a new day of social and economic justice and political freedom for Cuba.

Almost immediately, however, it appeared that Castro wanted to pick a quarrel with the United States. He refused to call free elections or to state firmly when he would do so. Communists moved into the key power positions in his government, in the police, the trade unions, the newspapers and radio. One after another of his early supporters resigned their government jobs and many left Cuba, charging that their revolution had been betrayed to the Communists.

Beginning in June 1959, the Castro government took over every part of Cuba's economic life—as the Communist governments had done in the countries of Eastern Europe. In what he called "government by television," Castro charged that the United States and private owners were guilty of many crimes against the Cuban people. He promised wealth to the poor, land to the landless.

But the take-over of agriculture, business and industry by men untrained to run them had mixed results. Many peasants were delighted to receive land of their own from the break-up of the plantations. New schools were built; new housing projects were begun. But many goods disappeared from the stores, wages were not paid, businesses closed. Agricultural cooperatives were formed but so far they have not been profitable. The disruption of the normal channels of trade and business, especially after the United States ceased to give Cuban sugar a preferred place in the American market, caused hardship and growing uncertainty.

There was no longer any question of Soviet intervention in Cuba when First Deputy Prime Minister Anastas Mikoyan traveled to Cuba in the spring of 1960 to buy large quantities of sugar. Shortly thereafter, when Castro was making one of his periodic outbursts about an imaginary American "invasion," Khrushchev threatened to repel American "aggression" against Cuba with rockets. Guevara, who had become Castro's closest advisor, went to Peking and returned with Communist China's promise to buy sugar. Hundreds of Russian and Chinese technicians and agents appeared in Cuba. Cuban embassies throughout Latin America became centers for the spread of Communist propaganda.

Castro himself, whether a Communist Party member or not, skillfully used every Communist device to keep himself in control—imprisoning and killing opponents, arming and drilling his people against invasion threats, whipping up hatred of the "imperialist" United States in inflammatory speeches, and censoring all sources of information to keep his people in ignorance of the facts.

Without doubt American mistakes of omission and commission have contributed to our difficulties in Cuba and in other parts of Latin America. Responsible men, inside and outside the government, have pointed these out to us and suggested remedies. It may be that the painful experience of Cuba will teach us and our Latin American friends how to prevent the Communist governments of the U.S.S.R. and China from enlarging their foot-hold in this hemisphere.

THE RULERS
AND THE RULED

6

The Rulers and The Ruled

The Communist Parties which today control the lives of almost a billion human beings are a small proportion of the people as a whole. The ratio of Party members to citizens in China is 1 in 130; in Russia 1 in 35; and in Czechoslovakia 1 in 10. Membership in the Communist Party is carefully chosen, for the Party admits to its ranks only men and women who have ability as leaders and organizers and who will accept its authority without question. The discipline demanded is severe but the rewards are very great.

The top jobs in industry, government, publishing, education—all these go to Party members. They have first choice of the all-too-scarce apartments, the few automobiles, the infrequent permission to make trips abroad. For the ambitious and aggressive young people there is no other road to advancement, for unlike the free countries, Communist countries have no independent institutions or organizations in which leadership can be practiced. Every institution and every organization is controlled by the Party.

Why, an American wonders, do the people accept this sharp division of society into rulers and ruled?

First of all, because they have no way to protest if the Party refuses to listen. Moreover, there is a constant, if small, improvement in living standards in the U.S.S.R. and its satellites (as yet this is not true in China). Each year there are better clothes in the stores, more TV sets for sale, more apartments to rent. (It is significant that the new apartments are built to provide kitchen and bathroom facilities only for several families together, so that people have a minimum of privacy.) People are grateful to their leaders for this visible improvement, for being much better off than they used to be, for educational and cultural opportunities which they formerly did not have.

Secondly, because they hold in their own hands control over everything their people read and hear, the Communist Parties believe they can mold the minds of their people to suit their program. Communist education of the children mirrors the purpose of the rulers. Unlike education in the United States which considers each child a unique individual, important for himself alone, Communist education is indoctrination and training in the service of the Communist regime. In the words of two Soviet educators,

> "Independence and initiative mean the display of the greatest self-denial and the readiness and ability to obey an order absolutely whatever the obstacles and dangers."

When the chairman of the department of pedagogics in the Leningrad Pedagogical Institute was asked, "What is morality in the U.S.S.R.?" he replied as follows:

> "Morality is a category of social conscience that is built within a student. The Communist state has very definite moral rules defining the kinds of attitudes and behaviors students should exhibit in matters involving labor, property, human relations and the role of the state. . . . Conformity to the basic moral rules and truths as defined by the Party is synonymous with morality in the U.S.S.R."

In the words of the Deputy Minister of Education of the Russian Soviet Federated Socialist Republic:

"The basic idea in moral education is to develop in them the ideal of society or the collective . . . It is important that children learn to subject their egoistic tendencies and feelings to the discipline of the collective."

Education in the lower grades is rapid and disciplined; critical thinking is discouraged, for fear it would weaken the acceptance of Party leadership and of Marxist-Leninist doctrine. Educational opportunities at the higher level are determined by the leaders. In the universities and higher schools of the U.S.S.R., for example, there are 290 specialties a student may study, but his choice is limited by the number of each which the Party wants in a certain year. If the Party wants more language specialists than chemists the would-be chemist must study linguistics. And vice versa. The young people of a Communist country are its tools in the economic and scientific competition with the Free World.

All teaching is under Party supervision. Textbooks are slanted to glorify the Communist leaders and system, and to create a false picture of the United States and the Free World. There are no open stacks in the libraries; specific books must be asked for and records kept of who reads what. All the newspapers of a Communist country print the same news stories. The same propaganda posters appear throughout the land. Since Western broadcasts are jammed and Western newspapers and magazines are almost impossible to obtain, the people have no way to judge the truth of what their governments tell them.

Will the System Change?

In the Soviet Union the Communist rulers apparently have their people's willing support. The regime's spectacular achievements in science and technology, shown by the sputniks, have given the people great pride in their country and themselves. As a goal for the future their leaders promise them an earthly paradise which they call "Communism." (As we have seen, they define the existing system as "socialism").

According to Khrushchev "Communism" is a state in the future, to be attained when "capitalism" and "imperialism" have ceased to exist. By promising that "Communism" will bring every earthly happiness, the Soviet leaders have given their people a reason for hard work and sacrifice. At the same time the Soviet people are encouraged to resist the "capitalist" and "imperialist" enemies —such as the United States—who, they say, block the attainment of "Communism."

Visitors to Russia have observed that the Soviet citizens make a distinction between the "imperialist ruling classes" of the United States and the "American people," whom they regard as unwilling victims of their rulers. Official Communist propaganda has made this distinction in the past, but in the December, 1960, declaration no distinction was made—the United States was declared the enemy. To what extent the Communist rulers can destroy the friendship which their subjects often feel for the "American people" will depend upon many factors, including our own words and actions.

In the Communist world where the threat of jail and deportation discourages opposition or doubt, it is impossible to tell how completely the rulers have succeeded in molding their people's minds. The refugees from East Germany, the uprisings in Poland and Hungary have showed that the degree of success varies. No one knows in 1961, for instance, whether the Chinese Communist leaders control the thoughts of their people as completely as they control their actions.

In the forty years since the Communist Revolution took place in Russia a new generation has grown up. Indoctrinated as they are in Marxism-Leninism, they are also better educated and better off than their parents who made the first

Revolution. They have built a society which they value and which they hope to preserve. This society would be devastated by nuclear war, as would ours. Many students of Communism believe that this new generation will be more willing to examine Communist "truths" critically and will demand a larger part in determining their own lives. Knowledge of the non-Communist world might hasten this process.

Contacts Work Both Ways

The dangers *to* the Free World of the Communist cultural and economic offensives are also opportunities *for* the Free World. The carefully planned and still limited exchanges of students and professional groups between Communist countries and the countries of the Free World hold promise of more knowledge on each side.

Admittedly the Communists use these exchanges to enforce their people's false and distorted picture of the "imperialist" world; this will continue to be so as long as Communist minds are imprisoned in Marxist-Leninist dogmas. But the writings of men like Djilas, Koestler and Leonhard, along with dozens of others, have made it clear that the Communist effort to black out the facts is never entirely successful. Some disturbing facts enter some Communist minds; some truths penetrate the jamming. The spread of education and the improvement of living standards have increased the number of people interested in the world beyond their Communist horizon.

On our part, these exchanges sharpen our knowledge of the tactics of the Communist rulers and enlarge our sympathy for those they rule. They may teach us something about the techniques of influencing men's minds—Communism's effective new instrument of conquest. They help us evaluate our own mistakes of omission and commission in our dealings with the Communist world.

Contacts between the Communist world and the so-called uncommitted nations have alarmed the Free World. This is understandable, since in many cases countries so wooed by the Communists have followed policies opposed to the United States in the United Nations and in the arena of world politics. It is often a mistake, however, to view these hostile policies as the result of Communist influence. The antagonism of many Arab countries to the West existed long before Khrushchev's trade deal with the United Arab Republic's President Nasser.

The Communist aid program is so new—only since 1954—that its long-range effect cannot yet be judged. In some countries of the Middle East, for example, closer acquaintance with Communist goods and Communist personnel has made Western goods and Western personnel attractive once more. Journalists and writers from non-Communist countries who are invited to the Soviet Union and Communist China often come back to criticize what they saw—several Indian journalists have done this of Communist China. African students paid to study in the Soviet Union have met racial discrimination there.

The increase of knowledge about Communist practices is not confined to the Free World but reaches every country which still has any freedom of communication. The excesses of Castro's Communist-dominated rule of Cuba have alarmed many Latin Americans who used to believe that the United States was unduly alarmed about the Communist threat. Since the Chinese conquest of Tibet the overseas Chinese have been less vulnerable to Communist propaganda.

In the battle for men's minds we may lack the concentration on destructive themes which the Communists use so effectively, but we have access to far a larger arsenal of facts. Our free press helps us see the world as it is; the Communists see it through the distortions of their own propaganda. We can learn from our mistakes for we acknowledge no central all-knowing authority which must be upheld at all costs. In the Free World regular elections make it possible to use new methods and enlist new people to meet our problems; we are not, like the Communists, at the mercy of one group of rulers.

We face a world of bewildering complexity and exciting challenge, in which knowledge is strength. The course of each country will be determined by many factors; the wisdom and training of its native leaders, its geography, resources and possibilities of economic development, the education and culture of its people, its internal problems and conflicts. Also of great importance are its past and present experience with the United States and other countries of the Free World, its relations with its neighbors, the skill of Communist propaganda and leadership. Policies suited to one country will not necessarily suit another. We have demanded for ourselves the right to make our own choices; we must honor and defend the same right for others.

An Old Challenge in a New Form

Today's Communist dictatorships are the newest form of a very old evil. The tyranny of the few over the many is as old as mankind. The lust for power and the corruptions of power are part of man. Each generation knows them in some form and conquers or is conquered by them.

Our generation confronts Communism. It is a global enemy with many faces. Marx equipped it with an ideology which offers promises of easy betterment to the poor and underprivileged. Lenin devised the instrument of the Communist Party, a tightly disciplined and autocratically-directed organization for seizing and maintaining power over the great majority of the people. He elaborated Marx's ideology to include the United States as an enemy to be overthrown by the world revolution. Stalin built the Soviet Union into a great military and industrial power. Under his dictatorship the Comintern perfected the technique of taking over countries by using Communist Parties to disrupt, infiltrate and capture. Khrushchev relies more upon propaganda than upon police methods in ruling his people but the secret police are still there. He uses trade, aid, and personal contacts with other world leaders in his efforts to persuade others to support Comnmuist purposes. Mao Tse Tung has driven the 650 million people of China into a rapid industrialization which he hopes will be an attractive example of Communism to other underdeveloped countries, and has unceasingly proclaimed his hostility to the United States.

But the Communist world has its own weaknesses. A system based on force and falsehood will always be threatened by the opposition of its subjects and by their glimpses of the truth. Millions of refugees from Communist countries —Germans, Hungarians, Tibetans, North Koreans, Chinese, Cubans, and others—are witnesses to the world of Communist tyranny.

Power struggles within each Communist Party and between the various Communist Parties will continue, for as Djilas says, "power is both the means and goal of Communists, in order that they may maintain their privileges and ownership." Conspiracy, falsehood and violence are among their habitual weapons. Communists fear and oppose reforms which will increase the stability and prosperity of countries they have marked for take-over. Each year more people understand the essence of contemporary Communism—power.

The Free World has its own strengths. Because it seeks to improve the lot of human beings as individuals, it can and does promote reforms. Because its economic system is made up of thousands of independent businesses and interests, it can—if it will—offer the underdeveloped peoples of the world more varied and more effective ways to build industry and technology. Because it encourages the formation and maintenance of freely elected governments, responsible to their peoples, it encourages the possibility of peaceful change and growth. Because it seeks a world in which human beings may make their own decisions, it can appeal to those who wish to be responsible for their own future. By its very existence, the Free World challenges Communist claims, for the United States and other democratically-governed countries have achieved a wider measure of human welfare and higher standards of living under free institutions than the Communist rulers have achieved by dictatorship.

Under the constant pressure of Communist aggression it is easy to lose sight of their weaknesses and our strengths. For centuries the Free World has fought the greatest enemies of all—proverty and misery—and in this battle the institutions of the Free World have a long head-start. Inspired by religions which teach that all men are brothers, men and women from the Free World have gone into the farthest corners of the earth on missions of service. In Asia, Africa, in Latin America, in the Middle East—everywhere in the world are schools, hospitals, colleges established by free people who have brought education, science, healing to those in need, regardless of nation or class. The Soviet Union has no Dr. Tom Dooley; Communist China has no Albert Schweitzer.

Since the second World War the nations of the Free World have aided less fortunate peoples in a manner and degree never before known to history, both as separate governments and through international agencies such as the United Nations Relief and Rehabilitation Agency, the World Health Organization, the Food and Agriculture Organization, the United Nations Children's Fund and others. Privately established foundations such as the Ford and Rockefeller Foundations are attacking basic problems by lending assistance in improving agriculture and training technical leadership. Through overseas branches of Free World business enterprises, thousands of people are learning the skills of technology. Universities offer scholarships to foreign students; schools exchange students and teachers; hospitals train doctors and technicians from other countries. Organizations like CARE, Meals for Millions, Save the Children, World Literacy and World Neighbors are lifting many out of hunger and ignorance.

In one important respect the Communists have an advantage over the Free World. Because they are centrally controlled, the decision for a particular policy need be made only by a few—it is then carried out by millions of disciplined and indoctrinated subjects. A decision by any country of the Free World requires the agreement of hundreds of individuals in parliaments and congresses and can only be as effective as the willingness of the citizens to carry it out. The triumph or defeat of the Communist threat depends on how thousands of individual citizens in the Free World choose to respond to it.

A Communist government can compel as many young people as it needs to study science and engineering. Will an adequate number in the Free World *choose* to do the same?

A Communist government can compel its technical experts to learn difficult foreign languages and live in remote parts of the world for indefinite periods. Will American, British, French, Canadian and other Free World experts *be willing* to do the same?

The Communist propaganda machine can broadcast to the world the big lie that the United States is the oppressor of the poor, of the Negroes, of other nations. How vigorously, how well do we counter their lies with *our deeds?*

No one can answer these questions, for the answers depend upon countless individual decisions now being made.

The Communist Parties hope to create the future in their own image, using their people as tools. The Free World hopes that the future will preserve and cherish the respect for individual human beings which has nurtured and protected us. Its success will depend upon the voluntary team-work of free men who understand the enemy and themselves.

By our individual decisions, each of us helps determine which future will prevail.

Glossary of Communist Terms

Words are regarded by Communists as weapons of conquest rather than as tools of thought, to create attitudes rather than to communicate exact ideas. Their meanings can and do change from time to time according to the purposes of the Communist leaders. The following definitions, therefore, can only describe previous and current uses of words by Communist authorities.

activist: Any citizen of a Communist country or member of a Communist Party who is particularly active in carrying out Communist purposes. The word implies that there are many citizens, even Party members, in Communist ranks who are content with a relatively passive role.

aggression: Lenin and his Communist followers claim that there are two kinds of wars, *just* wars fought to "liberate" countries they claim are "oppressed" in order to establish Communist governments; and "unjust" wars fought by any "imperialist" powers against each other or any Communist country. Only the "unjust" wars by the "imperialists" are "aggressive" wars and therefore only the "imperialist" or "capitalists" are capable of "aggression."

As Lenin declared in 1918: "The character of a war (whether reactionary or revolutionary) is not determined by who the aggressor was, or whose land the 'enemy' has occupied. It is determined by the class which is waging the war, and the politics of which the war is the continuation."

apparatus: The Party organization in a particular area. For instance, the Moscow apparatus is the Communist Party organization in Moscow.

bloc: From a French word meaning block or group. At present the term is used for a group of countries which acts more or less as a unit on matters of foreign policy, i. e., the Soviet bloc, the Western bloc.

Bolshevik: From the Russian word *bolshintsvo* meaning majority. Name given by Lenin to his faction in the Russian Social Democratic Party which voted in 1903 to become a secret, conspiratorial group. After 1912 the Bolshevik Party was a separate organization advocating revolution to overthrow capitalism. The members of the Russian Social Democratic Party who supported reform and political freedoms were called Mensheviks. After the Bolshevik Revolution of 1917 Lenin destroyed the Mensheviks as a political force. In 1919 the Bolshevik Party was renamed the Communist Party.

bourgeoisie: From the French word for townsman. "Bourgeoisie" is Marx's term for the merchant class which in the eighteenth century overthrew the French nobility and became the capitalist class. Although the change from feudalism to capitalism was peacefully accomplished in many countries, Marx argued that the violence which characterized the French Revolution was the rule in such change.

brain-washing: The combination of physical persecution and psychological pressures used by Communists to change the thinking of people in their power. The term was first used by the Chinese Comunists after their conquest of China. The practice is at least as old as the purges and show-trials in the U.S.S.R. in the 1930's.

capitalism: By Free World definitions, capitalism means the ownership of land and natural wealth, production, distribution and exchange of goods carried on by private enterprise and control under competitive conditions. The Communists claim that such private ownership and control enriches the owners at the expense of the workers and must be overthrown.

cell: The smallest unit of a Communist Party under strict control of higher Party officials.

Cheka: The secret police at the time of the Bolshevik Revolution and the Civil War. The secret police are an essential part of every Communist government because of the dictatorial nature of Communist rule. The Cheka was later called OGPU and still later MVD.

class struggle: In Marx's view of history, the "class struggle" was the struggle of the proletariat or working class against the "capitalists" in the separate countries. According to the December 1960 declaration of the world's Communist Parties the "class struggle" is the conflict between the Communist countries and their opponents, led principally by the United States.

collective leadership: Communist dictatorships have no legal processes by which leaders can be changed or by which new leaders can be chosen to replace those who die. Consequently there is always some degree of power struggle present in the Communist leadership, particularly when an acknowledged leader like Lenin or Stalin dies. In both cases the term "collective leadership" was used for a short period after their deaths and until the principal power had been concentrated in Stalin's and Khrushchev's hands.

colonialism: In the Free World, a colony means any distant territory dependent upon a ruling power and usually refers to the territories in Asia and Africa which became dependent upon European nations after the explorations and discoveries which began in the fifteenth century. Increasing resentment and opposition on the part of the peoples in the colonies resulted in the twentieth century in the freeing of most of them from dependence on their former rulers.

The term "colonialism" is widely used by Communist spokesmen to arouse hostility among the former colonies toward their former rulers.

In the Free World meaning of the word, the U.S.S.R. is the greatest of all colonial powers, holding millions of people in Eastern Europe in dependence. This fact is of little interest to Asians and Africans, however, where racial differences between rulers and ruled are regarded as the essence of "colonialism."

Comintern: The First International (1864-1876) and the Second International, founded in 1889 were working-class Socialist organizations. The Third International, founded at Moscow in 1919 under the leadership of Lenin and the Russian Communist Party, was composed of several national Communist Parties and organized to support the Bolshevik Revolution in Russia and promote the overthrow of "capitalist" governments everywhere. Usually referred to by the shortened name Comintern, it was officially declared dissolved by Stalin during World War II but its activities continued.

Cominform: When Yugoslavia under Tito began acting independently of Moscow Stalin organized the Cominform or Communist Information Bureau of world Communist Parties in order to bring organized Communist pressure against Tito. Although the Cominform was declared dissolved in 1956 in a period of Yugoslav-Soviet friendship, many other agencies exist to coordinate and control the activities of all Communist countries under Soviet influence.

communism: Sharing all goods in common as practiced by groups of early Christians and certain idealistic communities in the nineteenth century.

Communism: The term "Communism" was used by Marx to describe the condition of the world after the final overthrow of "capitalism" by the "dictatorship of the proletariat." Under "Communism," said Marx, "each would give according to his abilities, each would receive according to his needs." The word is still used by Communist leaders to describe the future when "capitalism" and "imperialism" have been eliminated.

According to the 1960 Declaration of the World Communist Party leaders, "Communism assures people freedom from fear of war, lasting peace, freedom from imperialist oppression and exploitation, from unemployment and poverty, general well-being and a high standard of living, freedom from fear of economic crises, a rapid growth of the productive forces for the benefit of society as a whole, freedom from the tyranny of the money bag over the individual, all-round spiritual development of man, the fullest development of talent, unlimited scientific and cultural progress of society."

As used in the Free World, Communism is the theory and practice of the communist Party or of any country or area under the control of members of a Communist Party. As the ex-Communist leader Milovan Djilas pointed out in *The New Class,* Communism takes somewhat different forms in different countries, but an essential aspect is always the totalitarian control of every aspect of life by the Communist Party dictatorship.

The careless use of the term "communism" to condemn people and policies with which we differ has drawn attention from actual Communist activity, both here and abroad, and confused many people about the nature, magnitude and complexity of the Communist challenge to the Free World.

Communist: A member of a Communist Party. Also an adjective referring to the policies and theories of Communist Parties and spokesmen.

Communist Party: The organization formed by Lenin to overthrow governments defined as "bourgeois" or "capitalist" and to maintain power over the states which they control. There are Communist Parties in at least eighty countries of the world but the activities of all are influenced and in most cases controlled from the U.S.S.R. Membership in a Communist Party is restricted and only men and women are admitted to Party membership whom the existing membership chooses. In a Communist-controlled country most of the positions of power and privilege are held by Party members. No organizations of any kind may exist except those controlled by the Communist Party. Percentage of Party members to the total population is small, varying from one in ten in Czechoslovakia to one in thirty-five in Communist China.

cult of personality: Or "cult of the individual." A term used by Khrushchev and other of Stalin's successors to explain the errors and crimes with which they charge Stalin. Although the attack on "the cult of the personality" and on Stalin was primarily launched to present the current leadership in a more attractive light, an effort was made to fit the attack into the Marxist theory that the masses, not individuals, are responsible for historical changes. The fact that this Marxist theory is the exact opposite of the Communist Party practice of a group of self-appointed non-removable rulers is but one of the many cases in which Marxist theory is one thing, Communist practice another.

democracy: The Communists used to make a distinction between "proletarian democracy" by which they meant a country ruled by the Communist Party supposedly on behalf of the proletariat, and "bourgeois democracy" which maintained free elections and freedom of speech and which they regarded as the last stage of decaying "capitalism." In the 1960 declaration of world Communist Parties this distinction is abandoned and the Communist system is called "democracy."

democratic centralism: In the early days of the Bolshevik Party, "democratic centralism" was declared by Lenin and other leaders to be the basis of Party organization and Communist leaders still claim that it is. According to their claims, Party bodies were supposed to be elected, Party leaders were supposed to be responsible to their membership, all lower Party organs must obey those above them, once a decision was announced all must obey without question.

In actual practice there has been neither election of leaders nor responsibility of leaders to membership in the various Communist Parties. "Democratic centralism" really means authoritarian rule from above demanding unquestioned obedience.

dialectic: The theory that human development takes place in cycles of change, originally stated by Hegel, adopted by Marx.

dialectical materialism: Marx's explanation of history and the reasons for history. The philosophical basis of Communist doctrine and the framework into which Communist spokesmen endeavor to fit their actions. Marx's theory of history as change brought about by the "class struggle."

dictatorship of the working class (proletariat): This term was first used by Marx in 1875 to describe the form the state would take in the revolutionary period of change from Capitalism into Communism. In 1920 Lenin wrote: "The revolutionary dictatorship of the proletariat is power won and maintained by the violence of the proletariat against the bourgeoisie, power that is unrestricted by any laws." In 1956 a Soviet spokesman wrote that "Marxism holds that the essence of the socialist revolution in the transition period under all conditions is the dictatorship of the proletariat. The parliamentary road to Socialism is impossible without the establishment of this dictatorship." Since from the beginning Communists have claimed that the "dictatorship of the proletariat" is identical with the "dictatorship of the Communist Party"—it is clear that "dictatorship of the Communist Party" is the essential element in Communist purpose and practice.

freedom: In the standard Soviet dictionary freedom is defined as "the recognition of necessity." A free person is someone who accepts the Party's policies as right. A similar twisting of meaning is found in the discussion of "independence" and "initiative" by two Soviet educators, who write: "Independence and initiative mean the display of the greatest self-denial and the readiness and ability to obey an order absolutely whatever the obstacles and dangers."

This distortion of meanings explains the difficulty citizens of the Free World have in their occasional encounters with Soviet citizens.

Although Soviet leaders have to a large extent succeeded in stamping these definitions on the minds of their own people, they have not been so successful in countries taken over by Communists, such as Poland, Hungary, East Germany and so on.

front: Communist term to describe an organization which pretends to pursue a desirable objective, such as "world peace," but is actually used by Communist leadership to promote

Communist policies. In addition to organizations formed by Communists themselves some originally democratic organizations have become "fronts" when Communist members of the organization have obtained key positions.

imperialism: As used by Lenin and his followers "imperialism" means the establishment of business and trade relations by citizens of capitalist nations with other countries. Since, according to Lenin, "capitalist" use the labor of other men solely for their own profit, the word "imperialism" suggests that "capitalism" countries, including the United States, start businesses and carry on trade with people of other countries in order to enrich themselves at those people's expense.

kulak: The more prosperous farmers of the early days of the Bolshevik Revolution, systematically exterminated by Stalin.

materialism: Marx's theory, accepted by Communists, that men's motives are entirely economic and materialistic by nature, ideas and ideals being only a reflection of material conditions and goals.

Menshevik: From Russian word for minority, the name given to the wing of the Russian Social Democratic Party which in 1903 split from Lenin's Bolsheviks over the decision to form a conspiratorial, revolutionary Party. The Mensheviks favored reform and political freedoms and were finally destroyed as a political force by Lenin in 1918.

morality: According to Lenin and current Soviet spokesmen, "morality" is what promotes Communism as defined by Communist leaders. In the words of two leading Soviet educators: "Communist morality is morality of a new, higher type. The struggle for the construction of Communism is its basis. To be a moral person means to build Communism actively, to give all your strength and energy to the building of a Communist society . . ."

movement: A propaganda and pressure campaign undertaken by the Chinese Communist government to compel its people to carry out a particular policy of the Communist leadership.

national-liberation: Term used extensively in the December 1960 declaration of Communist Parties to describe the change from colonial to independent status by many countries in Africa and Asia. Communist spokesmen have welcomed "national-liberation" as a transition stage before the establishment of the Communist controlled system of "socialism."

peace: The absence of class war, in other words, the conditions where the "bourgeois" and "capitalist" states have been replaced by Communist states.

peaceful coexistence: According to the 1960 declaration of world Communist parties, "peaceful coexistence" means the continuation of the "class struggle" by other than military means. "In conditions of peaceful coexistence favorable opportunities are provided for the development of the class struggle in the capitalist countries and the national-liberation movement of the peoples of the colonial and dependent countries. In their turn the successes of the revolutionary class and national-liberation struggle promote peaceful coexistence."

people's democracy: A term invented after World War II to describe the Communist-controlled systems of the countries in Eastern Europe and regarded as the stage *before* a Communist-controlled "socialism."

purge: Removal by banishment, show trial or murder of those suspected of opposition to the group in power in a Communist state. In a one-party state without free elections, purges are the only means of dealing with opposition to the leadership. Under Communist control there will always be purges.

proletariat: The industrial working-class in the "capitalist" societies which developed as a result of the Industrial Revolution.

reactionary: Originally Communists used this term to refer to "capitalists" or supporters of "capitalism" who opposed the Communist program of revolution and take-over. It is now used by the Communists in power to condemn other Communists whom they wish to displace or weaken.

rehabilitation: Three years after Stalin's death, in 1956, his successors announced that he had killed many loyal Communists on false charges of treason. These men were declared to be "rehabilitated," in other words, they were proclaimed to have been loyal Communists after all.

revisionism: Any Communist country or group of Communists who follow policies or programs other than those laid down by the Soviet leaders in Moscow is accused of "revisionism." Since any independence on the part of Communist Parties or Party members weakens the power of the Soviet Communist Party over all other Parties, "revisionism" is a serious Communist sin. In the 1960 declaration Yugoslavia was condemned for its "revisionism."

scientific: The adjective "scientific" is used by Communists to distinguish Marx's political and social theories from all others. They hope to borrow the prestige of science for what are after all unproved and unprovable theories, and therefore in no sense scientific.

Social Democrat (or Socialist): Member of a party which advocates government ownership of the principal means of production within the framework of political freedoms such as free elections and free speech. Under various names (Labor Party in Great Britain, Socialist Party in the United States) there are Social Democrat or Socialist Parties in most of the countries of the Free World. They advocate change through orderly free political institutions and are fiercely opposed by the Communists because they command the loyalty of large numbers of workingmen whom the Communists claim to represent. The planned destruction of the Socialist or Social Democratic parties in the countries of Eastern Europe and in China was an essential step in the Communist takeover of those countries. In the December 1960 declaration the Communist leaders accused the Socialist parties of being "reformist" and attacked them for having "done a service to the bourgeoisie."

Socialism: As used by the Social Democrat and Socialist Parties of the Free World socialism means government ownership and control of the principal means of production if and when the people in free elections vote for such ownership and control. Strictly speaking all participation by government in economic activity is socialistic, so that federal loans to buy or build houses, social security, government irrigation and flood control projects, control of utility rates and so on are socialistic. The degree of socialism in the Free World varies from country to country and from time to time. The term a "Socialist" correctly applies only to those who support government ownership of the principal means of production.

"Socialism": As used by Communists "socialism" means government ownership and control of *all* economic activity under the complete and single domination of the Communist Party, which also controls the government, the press, radio and television, education, the entire life of its citizens.

Socialist camp: The group of countries controlled by Communist Parties. Yugoslavia is sometimes included in this term, sometimes not.

socialist realism: That quality in art or literature which the Party believes promotes the ideals of a Communist society. Since the Party defines these ideals, it also defines what kind of art and literature is acceptable in a Communist country. There is no freedom for an artist or writer to create what he wishes in the Soviet Union or in Communist China, but in some of the satellite countries considerable freedom is now and then exercised.

Suggested Reading

The following books are recommended because they are readable, authoritative, and available, many of them appearing in paper-back editions. Those readers who wish further suggestions among the hundreds of books on all aspects of Communism should consult school or public libraries or write the Foreign Policy Association, World Affairs Center, United Nations Plaza at 47th Street, New York.

Communist China and Asia, A. Doak Barnett, Harper & Brothers, New York, 1960.

The Future Is Ours, Comrade, Joseph Novak, Doubleday & Co., Inc., New York, 1950.

The God That Failed, edited by Richard Crossman, Harper & Brothers, New York, 1960.

How the Soviet System Works, Raymond A. Bauer, Alex Inkeles and Clyde Kluckhohn, Random House, New York, 1960.

Masters of Deceit, J. Edgar Hoover, Holt, Rinehart & Winston, Inc., New York, 1957.

Neither War Nor Peace: The Struggle for Power in The Post-War World, Hugh Seton-Watson, Frederick A. Praeger, Inc., New York, 1960.

The New Class, Milovan Djilas, Frederick A. Praeger, Inc., New York, 1957.

Russia and The West Under Lenin and Stalin, George F. Kennan, Little Brown & Co., Boston, 1961.

Stalin: A Political Biography, Isaac Deutscher, Random House, New York, 1960.

Three Who Made A Revolution, Bertram Wolfe, The Dial Press, Inc., New York, 1948.

To The Finland Station, Edmund Wilson, Harcourt Brace & Co., New York, 1940.

To Moscow and Beyond: A Reporter's Narrative, Harrison Salisbury, Harper & Brothers, New York, 1960.

Index

G

H

K

L

O-P

T